THE MATHESON MONOGRAPHS

The principal objective of the Matheson Trust is to promote the study of comparative religion from the point of view of the underlying harmony of the great religious and philosophical traditions of the world. This objective is being pursued through such means as audio-visual media, the support and sponsorship of lecture series and conferences, the creation of a website, collaboration with film production companies and publishing companies as well as the Trust's own series of publications.

The Matheson Monographs will cover a wide range of themes within the field of comparative religion: scriptural exegesis in different religious traditions; the modalities of spiritual and contemplative life; in-depth mystical studies of particular religious traditions; broad comparative analyses taking in a series of religious forms; studies of traditional arts, crafts and cosmological sciences; and contemporary scholarly expositions of religious philosophy and metaphysics. The monographs will also comprise translations of both classical and contemporary texts as well as transcriptions of lectures by, and interviews with, spiritual and scholarly authorities from different religious and philosophical traditions.

ORPHEUS AND THE ROOTS OF PLATONISM

ORPHEUS

AND

THE ROOTS
OF PLATONISM

Algis Uždavinys

THE MATHESON TRUST
For the Study of Comparative Religion

© The Matheson Trust, 2011

The Matheson Trust
PO Box 336
56 Gloucester Road
London SW7 4UB, UK

www.themathesontrust.org

ISBN: 978 1 908092 07 6 paper

British Library Cataloguing-in-Publication Data.
A catalogue record for this book is
available from the British Library

Cover: Detail from a Graeco-Roman vase, 2nd-3rd century CE.

CONTENTS

Preface . . . .*ix*

I. A Model of Unitive Madness. 1

II. Socratic Madness 5

III. Socrates as Seer and Saviour 9

IV. Philosophy, Prophecy, Priesthood. 17

V. Scribal Prophethood. 19

VI. Eastern and Greek Prophethood. 21

VII. Inside the Cultic Madness of the Prophets 25

VIII. Egyptian Priesthood 32

IX. Orpheus as Prophet 37

X. Orpheus and the Pythagorean Tradition 41

XI. Orpheus and Apollo 44

XII. The Orphic Revolution 47

XIII. Knowledge into Death. 52

XIV. Telestic Restoration. 58

XV. The Lyre of Orpheus. 61

XVI. The Cosmic Unfolding of the One 64

XVII. Recollection and Cyclic Regression 68

XVIII. Orphic and Platonic Forms 72

XIX. The Method of Philosophical Catharsis 76

XX. Deification of the Egyptian Initiate-Philosopher. . . 79

XXI. From Homer to Hermetic Secrecy 84

XXII. Into the Mysteries 89

XXIII. Beyond the Tomb 93

XXIV. Conclusion 97

PREFACE

The present book is closely related to that famous Pre-Socratic fragment about the bow and the lyre, where their "back-stretched" or "retroflex" harmony (*palintonos harmonia*) is said to depict the tense inner cohesion of a diverging unity. The same authority, Heraclitus of Ephesus, employs a Greek pun to show how in the bow itself, one of whose names is *bios*, both the name of life and the act of death coexist. Orpheus, as a mythical hero—indeed, one of the famed Argonauts—stands right at the centre of these junctions. So it is no wonder that this book shares in that harmonious tension: a tension rooted in the nature of the lyre and the bow, whose products may be piercing sounds or slaying arrows.

Here, we have first a tension within the author, who is intoxicated with his theme and yet committed to carry out his exposition in a discursive and academic manner. We can almost feel his plight: having in mind the "tremendous contemplation of the divine truth and beauty", which would merit either a *bakchic* outburst or a "supra-noetic metaphysical silence", he is forcing himself to compose a "scientific" treatise. Having heard the music of Orpheus' lyre, he is trying to convey as best as he can the unspeakable beauty of those notes in an all too earthly human language.

Second, as a direct consequence of the first, there is tension for the reader as he tries to follow the argument itself: strands of myth and mythic lore mix with dense epistemological and metaphysical discussion; abstruse Egyptian and Babylonian sources stand next to conventional Greek philosophical and 21st century academic references. The thing is said, yet not fully; inadequately expressed with an almost deliberate disdain for exactitude on a plane which becomes redundant in the light of spiritual vision. This book moves uneasily between the apophatic and the cataphatic: trying to say something, saying something, hinting at something else, then finally keeping silent, finding itself lost for words, leaving the doors thrown open to a different understanding.

Then we find a third sort of tension, springing from the duality at the heart of the subject: Orpheus is a strange hero, one who has music and singing for weapons. He is a seer and tragic lover, yet a crucial figure in the history of philosophy. His place in the history of Greek religion and thought is still, even in specialised circles, something of a riddle, enigmatic and vague.

This book, densely packed with references, challenges, and subtle invitations, is a recapitulation or a critical reassessment of ancient and contemporary literature devoted to Orpheus, the "paradigmatic itinerant seer", "the Theologian", "the Saviour". It gives special attention to his relations with both the Egyptian and the Platonic tradition. At the heart of this book we have a glimpse into the substance, nature and development of the Orphic mysteries, but the reader must be warned: this is not a history of Orphism, and this is no ordinary scholarly monograph. Those who approach this book with respect for the ancient mysteries, humbly trying to understand why our ancestors across cultures unfailingly gave to Plato the epithet of "Divine" (*Divus Plato*, or *Aflatun al-Ilahi*, as the Arabs used to call him), hoping for that "epistemic and hermeneutical illumination mediated by the holy light of myths and symbols," such will find a treasure here: not a wealth of answers to be sure, but a wealth of mystagogic insights and intimations, sparks perhaps of that "fiery beauty of truth" contemplated by the author.

The brief earthly transit of Algis Uždavinys started in Lithuania in 1962. He completed his studies in Vilnius, graduating from the former State Art Institute of Lithuania, now Vilnius Academy of Fine Arts, where he would eventually become head of the Department of Humanities. Uždavinys was widely respected as a prolific author in Lithuania and abroad. He was renowned as a translator into Russian and Lithuanian of Ancient Egyptian and Greek texts, of Traditionalist works by Frithjof Schuon and Martin Lings, and he was active as well as an art critic and author of numerous articles and monographs (a list of his books can be found at the end of this volume). His interest in traditional doctrines would eventually take him around the world and to Jordan and Egypt, where he met living representatives of the Prophetic chain of wisdom embodied in the Qur'an and the Sunna. These would foster and orient his research projects until his untimely death in 2010. Not long before his passing and after he had completed this, his final book, he told his wife: "I have nothing else to say." As someone who devoted his life to the understanding and cultivation of the Divine, Algis Uždavinys must surely be taken as evidence of the ancient Greek saying "whom the Gods love, die young."

Like the Homeric epics, the current work is formed by twenty-four untitled chapters. Given the character of the book, less informative than mystagogic, and less systematic than symphonic, we have preferred to leave the brief chapters as they are, adding titles for ease of reference only in the table of contents.

Five major sections may be discerned in the book: chapters I-III deal with inspired madness in general, and with Socratic mania in particular; IV-VIII with the relations between philosophy, prophecy and priesthood, considering Middle Eastern, Egyptian and Greek traditions in general; chapters IX-XII narrow the scope to the figure of Orpheus as a prophet, considering his place in the Pythagorean tradition and in the development of Greek philosophy; chapters XIII-XVII touch on some of the deepest aspects of Orphic symbolism, considering the Orphic *bakcheia* (initiatic rites) and way of life (the *bios Orphikos*); chapters XVIII-XXII relate all the above to the history of Greek wisdom-philosophy, from Homer down to Hermeticism with special attention to Plato's theories and their Egyptian associations. The book concludes with a chapter on the realities beyond the tomb (XXIII), followed by a surrender of all arguments and a moving self-disclosure (XXIV). Silence reigns pregnant with mystical resonance.

Juan Acevedo
Director
The Matheson Trust

ORPHEUS AND THE ROOTS
OF PLATONISM

*Melancholy and the awakening of one's genius are inseparable, say
the texts. Yet for most of us there is much sadness and little genius,
little consolation of philosophy, only the melancholic stare—what to
do, what to do. . . . Here our melancholy is trying to make knowledge, trying to see through. But the truth is that the melancholy is the
knowledge; the poison is the antidote. This would be the senex's most
destructive insight: our senex order rests on senex madness. Our order is itself a madness.*[1]

* * *

*To this we may add the conclusion. It seems that, whether there is or
is not a one, both that one and the others alike are and are not, and
appear and do not appear to be, all manner of things in all manner
of ways, with respect to themselves and to one another.*[2]

I

In Plato's *Phaedrus*, Socrates argues paradoxically that "our
greatest blessings come to us by way of madness" (*ta megista
ton agathon hemin gignetai dia manias*: *Phaedr.* 244a). The four

---

1. *The Essential James Hillman: A Blue Fire*, introduced and edited by
Thomas Moore (London: Routledge, 1994), pp. 212 & 215.

2. Plato, *Parmenides* 166b. tr. F. M. Cornford, *The Collected Dialogues of
Plato*, ed. Edith Hamilton and Huntington Cairns (Princeton: Princeton
University Press, 1989), p. 956.

kinds of divine inspiration, or madness, are viewed as a divine gift provided by the Muses, Dionysus, Apollo and Aphrodite (or Eros) respectively. In the same dialogue, the "divine banquet" is depicted as a metaphysical place of contemplation and vision. For Plato, the contemplation (*theoria*) of the eternal Ideas transcends our rational ability to comprehend and analyse these Ideas discursively.

The desperate longing for this paradigmatic contemplation is imagined as a yearning for wings and the regained ability to fly to the divine banquet. Accordingly, this pressing desire is the desire for wholeness, for noetic integrity, and for one's true divine identity provided by dialectical searching, philosophical recollection and erotic madness. The hierarchically organized troops of gods are led by Zeus. They lack both jealousy and passion, being involved neither in plots, nor in heavenly wars:

> The gods have no need for madness, let alone erotic madness; hence the gods are not philosophers. It is not surprising, then, that the gods seem to have no need for *logos* (let alone for rhetoric). Although there is a certain amount of noise in the heavens, there is no reference whatsoever to there being any discourse among the gods or between gods and men.[3]

Therefore the Platonic philosopher, as the madman who nurtures wings, is the dialectically transformed "speaker" (the fallen soul encharmed by the magic of *logos*) whose apparently mad desire and *erotike mania* are not so much directly sent from the gods as sparkling from within as a desire for the divine banquet and for wisdom. But the three other kinds of madness discussed in Plato's *Phaedrus*, namely, poetic (*poietike mania*) telestic (*telestike mania*), and prophetic or mantic madness (*mantike mania*) indeed are sent by the gods.

---

3. Charles L. Griswold, *Self-Knowledge in Plato's Phaedrus* (New Haven and London: Yale University Press, 1989), p. 97.

The Muses are specified as the source of the poetic inspiration and of the three forms of madness; "the poetic sort seems to be the closest to Socratic-Platonic philosophizing and hence to be its most complex antagonist," as Charles Griswold remarks.[4]

The telestic madness is anagogic, and leads the soul to its forgotten origins through the theurgic rites of ascent or other sacramental means of purification. The inspired telestic liturgies (*telestike, hieratike telesiourgia, theophoria*) are not necessarily to be regarded straightforwardly as "operations on the gods", thus deliberately and incorrectly equating the animated cultic statues located in the context of particular ritual communications with the invisible metaphysical principles themselves. Otherwise, tacitly or not, the polemical premises for a certain iconoclastic bias are maintained. And so H.J. Blumenthal puts too much weight on the verb *theourgein*, supposing that one who does *theia erga* is one who operates on the gods, thereby making theurgy a nonsense.[5]

The mantic inspiration, or prophetic madness, which allegedly produces countless benefits, is evoked and evidenced, first of all, by the prophetesses at Delphi, thus recalling the close connection between the Apollonian shrine at Delphi and the philosophical self-knowledge required by Plato's Socrates. According to Griswold, "Socratic prophecy seems to combine the human techne of division or dissection with the divinely given techne of madness; that is, it somewhat combines . . . madness and sophrosyne."[6]

The Apollonian prophecy is inseparable from philosophizing and, hence, from rhetoric in its expanded general sense, showing and leading souls by persuasion or imperative—like a sacrificial priest, using the dialectical art of definition, divi-

---

4. *Ibid.*, p. 77.

5. H.J. Blumenthal, "From ku-ru-so-wo-ko to theougos: word to ritual," in *Soul and Intellect: Studies in Plotinus and Later Platonism* (Aldershot: Ashgate, Variorum, 1993), XI, p. 6.

6. Charles L. Griswold, *ibid.*, p. 76.

sion and collection. Yet neither is the sacrificer to be viewed as a paradigm of theological understanding, nor the user of the art of rhetoric made subject to his own enchanting power of persuasion. However, they may become types of self-duped "believers" or acquire the ideologically tinctured, and therefore very "orthodox", ability to talk about "truth"—or virtually any subject—and so become "difficult to be with". As Griswold correctly observes, Plato's Socrates

> seems to fear the canonization of a *biblos*. That is, the written word lets us *persuade* ourselves too easily that we are in irrefutable possession of the truth, while in fact we are not. It facilitates our tendency to become dogmatists or zealots rather than philosophers. . . . Under these conditions philosophy can have the same corrupting influence that sophistry does or worse.[7]

However, academic paranoia differs from prophetic madness. The so-called prophets (*theomanteis, manteis theoi,* or Aristotle's *sibullai kai bakides kai hoi entheoi pantos*: *Probl.* 954a.36) fall into *enthusiasmos*, the state of a particular "inspired ecstasy", and utter truths of which they themselves presumably know nothing. Hence, being *entheos* means that the body has a god or a *daimon* within, just as the Egyptian animated statue has a manifestation (*ba*) of a god (*neter*) within. Similarly, *empsuchos* means that both the physical human body and the cultic body (the hieratic statue or the entire sanctuary, itself full of images, statues and hieroglyphs) have an animating, life-giving and self-moving principle—namely, a soul (*psuche*)—inside them.

Orpheus is an example of one who has all these four kinds of inspiration or madness according to Hermeias the Alexandrian Neoplatonist, whose commentary on Plato's *Phaedrus* reflects the views of his master Syrianus.[8] Since these four *ma-*

---

7. *Ibid.*, pp. 207 & 208.
8. Anne Sheppard, *The Influence of Hermeias on Marsilio Ficino's Doctrine*

niai assist the soul in its ascent and return to its noetic father-land, Hermeias maintains that poetry and music are able to bring the disordered parts of the soul into order. The hieratic rites and sacramental mysteries of Dionysus make the soul whole and noetically active. Subsequently, the prophetic in-spiration (*mantike mania*) is provided by Apollo and gathers the soul together into its own unity.

Hermeias regards the charioteer in the *Phaedrus* myth as the noetic part of the soul and the charioteer's head as the "one within the soul", or the soul's ineffable henadic summit which alone may be united with the One. Thus, finally, as Anne Sheppard explains, "the inspiration of love takes the unified soul and joins the one within the soul to the gods and to intelligible beauty."[9]

II

Perhaps with a certain measure of irony, Socrates was viewed by the majority of Athenians as a chatterer, an idle talker (*alolesches*). But this alleged idle talker obeyed and followed his god Apollo. He philosophized in the streets on the god's behalf, and preached a kind of "spiritual pederasty" that leads the lovers (*eirastes*) of youths to the ideocentric love of Platonic truth and beauty. In this respect, Socrates is neither a "typical representative of the Greek Enlightenment", nor the "intellectual leader of Athenian intellectuals", as influen-tial Western scholars would claim until recently, ". . . nor did he discourse, like most others, about the nature of the uni-verse, investigating what the experts call 'cosmos'. . . . Those who did so he showed up as idiots," according to Xenophon (*Mem.* 1.1.11).

---

of Inspiration, Journal of the Warburg and Courtauld Institutes, 43, 1980, p. 105.

9. *Ibid.,* p. 106.

Initially acting as a typical idle talker, Socrates realizes himself as a moralist. Strictly speaking, the man who is persuaded by nothing in him except the proposition which appears to him the best when he reasons about it (*Crit.* 46b) is no metaphysician either, though Apollo commanded him (as he "supposed and assumed") to live philosophizing, examining himself and others (*Ap.* 28e). Socrates saw his own work in "philosophizing", that is, in summoning all citizens (but especially wealthy youths of aristocratic origins) to perfect their soul, as a sort of socio-political mission following the god's command and acting on the god's behalf. Therefore, his performance of thus understood "dialectical" work (*ergon*) can be imagined as a form of piety in service (*latreia*) to the god. Gregory Vlastos argues:

> Were it not for that divine command that first reached Socrates through the report Chaerepon brought back from Delphi there is no reason to believe that he would have ever become a street philosopher. If what Socrates wants is partners in elenctic argument, why should he not keep to those in whose company he had sought and found his eudaimonist theory—congenial and accomplished fellow seekers after moral truth? Why should he take to the streets, forcing himself on people who have neither taste nor talent for philosophy, trying to talk them into submitting to a therapy they do not think they need?[10]

There is no explanation other than a supposed divine command (be it just literary *topos* or some inner experience) or Socrates' own wild presumption, keeping in mind that Socrates was no mystic in any conventional religious sense, but rather a zealous social worker and rationalizing moralist serving his god for the benefit of his fellow Athenians. This

---

10. Gregory Vlastos, *Socratic Piety*, ed. Gail Fine (Oxford: Oxford University Press, 2000), pp. 558-59.

"madman's theatre" is nevertheless regarded as a revolution-
ary project: "

> And it is of the essence of his rationalist programme in the-
> ology to assume that the entailment of virtue by wisdom
> binds gods no less than men. He could not have tolerated
> a double-standard morality, one for men, another for the
> gods. . . . Fully supernatural though they are, Socrates' gods
> could still strike his pious contemporaries as rationalist fab-
> rications. . . . [11]

Socrates undoubtedly regarded his own "rationalism" and
his leap from epistemological ignorance to public political
and moral expertise as devised by the *daimonion*, the super-
natural guide. His own front door was adorned, as A.H. Armstrong relates, by "an unshaped stone called Apollo of the
Ways and another stone called a Herm with a head at the top
and a phallus halfway down, which Socrates would tend at
the proper time like every other Athenian householder".[12]

In this respect he was quite traditional, although his presumably esoteric side (if this curious aspect of Socrates is
not invented by Plato's dramatic imagination) is close to the
madness of Orpheus, the divinely inspired mythical singer.
In the context of traditional Hellenic culture, Orphism and
Pythagoreanism may be viewed as a "small sectarian movement". Alternatively, Orphism may be presented as a new
spiritual programme of radically revised anthropology and
of both cosmic and personal soteriology, partly derived from
Egyptian and Anatolian sources. In either case, the Orphic
doctrines sharply differ from those of early Hellenic (the so-
called Homeric and pre-Homeric) spirituality.

---

11. *Ibid.*, pp. 545 & 547.

12. A.H. Armstrong, "The Ancient and Continuing Pieties of the Greek
World," in *Classical Mediterranean Spirituality: Egyptian, Greek, Roman*, ed.
A.H. Armstrong (London: Routledge & Kegan Paul, 1986), p. 68.

The main Orphic doctrine follows the pattern already established in the *Pyramid Texts*, asserting that the royal soul has its goal in unity with the divine through ascent and recollection. With considerable modifications, this anagogic scenario became an integral part of Platonism, whose adherents practised rising up to the heights of philosophical contemplation through the anagogic power of *eros*, and were able to reach the noetic Sun by a combination of dialectical and telestic means. In short, Orphism maintained that the human soul is immortal and is subject to divine judgement:

> The divine in us is an actual being, a *daimon* or spirit, which has fallen as a result of some primeval sin and is entrapped in a series of earthly bodies, which may be animal and plant as well as human. It can escape from the "sorrowful weary wheel", the cycle of reincarnation, by following the Orphic way of life, which involved, besides rituals and incantations, an absolute prohibition of eating flesh. . . . [13]

The somewhat clumsy Socrates hardly fits the much demanding Orphic ideals, although he nevertheless functions in Plato's *Symposium* as an Orpheus figure, being presented as a literary double of *Phanes*. The self-manifested Phanes of the Orphic cosmogonies should be described as *Protogonos* (the first-born, tantamount to the noetic light which appears from the egg of ineffable darkness), whose other name is the demiurgic Eros.[14] He carries within himself the seed of the gods and copulates with himself like the Egyptian *Atum*.

Sara Rappe emphasizes "the centrality of Orphic symbolism in the *Symposium* as a whole", arguing that there is good reason to attribute the allegorizing use of Orphic material to

---

13. *Ibid.*, p. 99.
14. Sara Rappe, *Reading Neoplatonism: Non-discursive thinking in the texts of Plotinus, Proclus, and Damascius* (Cambridge: Cambridge University Press, 2000), p. 150.

Plato himself, and not only to Syrianus, Proclus, Damascius or Olympiodorus. She says:

> The Orphic mystery purports to be an esoteric tradition, one that liberates people from the petrifying conventions of the mass sex-gender machine. Its purpose is to re-create the subject, to wrench him away from the public fiction in which he has hitherto been schooled. . . . The Orphic myth promises a return to the undifferentiated state before sexual identity arises, promising to deliver us back inside the egg to become in the Lacanian sense, hommelettes. But of course, this is a delusional aspiration, as the myth makes clear, and it is in fact a self-destructive delusion. . . . In my reading of the Orphic cosmology in Plato's *Symposium*, I have emphasized its function as an etiology for human consciousness, prior to its regeneration by philosophy. This is the exoteric mind that desperately requires enlightenment but because of its conditioning, all too rarely seeks it.[15]

III

The alleged correspondences between Socrates and Orpheus, or rather, between Plato and Orpheus, are explored by Proclus, to whom an esoteric interpretation of Plato's dialogues is tantamount to the initiatory Orphic doctrine. Accordingly, the Orphic *Phanes* (like the Egyptian *Atum-Ra*) shows forth the soul as an image (*eikon*) of the shining divine Intellect. The recognition of the pharaonic *imago dei* (*tut neter* in the Egyptian royal theology) and of its restored Osirian wholeness (the right Eye of Horus made sound) itself constitutes a sort of initiation that enables the soul's access to the divine realm.

Rappe claims that since the time of Syrianus, either Orphism is attached to metaphysics in order to transform the

---

15. *Ibid.*, pp. 152 & 155.

Neoplatonic doctrine into ritual, or the language of meta-physics is grafted on to a traditional Orphic narrative.[16] However, such theurgic convergency is initially based on Egyptian hermeneutical and cultic patterns. She argues as follows:

> The "Rhapsodic Theogony" ends with a famous hymn to Zeus, in which his identity as the *coincidentia oppositorum* is revealed. . . . This vision of the world of Zeus gives us a kind of mirror of the Proclan universe, in which each being is an all, and all beings are in each. . . . The multiple states of being, each level mutually reflecting all of the others, proliferate as a hall of mirrors. It is this great world of mutual interpenetration endlessly expanding as a single drama, that the Orphic theogony captures. And not surprisingly, this vision is exactly the mythic equivalent of Proclus' central metaphysical views.[17]

Proclus' assertion that all Hellenic theology ultimately derives from Orphic mystagogy (*Plat. Theol.* I.5.25)[18] may be regarded as a normative and paradigmatic claim of his philosophical hermeneutics. Thus, Orpheus constitutes the archetypal mark of his metaphysical topography. In this particular sense, the name and image of Orpheus function more like the theological *arche*, like the canonized philosophical *hupostasis*, than as an unquestioned and factual person of ancient history. This imaginative assertion of Proclus, though belonging to the realm of semi-mythic genealogies, is shared by the countless followers of the ancient Hellenic tradition and constitutes one of its main etiological kernels. Consequently, it is this image of the esoteric Orpheus that counts, not one provided by the modern academic interpretations that present

---

16. *Ibid.*, p. 164.

17. *Ibid.*, p. 160.

18. Algis Uždavinys, Introduction, *The Golden Chain: An Anthology of Pythagorean and Platonic Philosophy*, ed. Algis Uzdavinys (Bloomington, IN: World Wisdom, 2004), pp. XXIV-XXV.

their hypothetical contructions as an ultimate truth about a given tradition in place of the self-representations, theological images and myths used by adherents of the tradition.

For the late Platonic tradition, the "fighters"—those belonging to the "sacred race" (*hiera genea*)—defend, according to Syrianus, "the best and most beautiful of philosophies", namely, the Kronian way of life (*In Metaph.* 91.8ff).[19] These intellectual defenders of tradition recognized themselves as forming a link in a golden Platonic chain, claiming that inwardly all human beings are divine and, therefore, must become conscious of this inherent divinity. The anagogic tradition of a journey within consists in an unbroken chain of divinely inspired teachers, who both taught and practised the revealed Platonic mysteries. As Polymnia Athanassiadi remarks:

> In a society in which political propagandists had raised the principle of imperial legitimacy to a metaphysical level, the Neoplatonists came effortlessly to evolve and spread a dynastic theology. Indeed by the time of Damascius, the history of the caste had acquired its own mythology as well, for the creation of which all sorts of forged genealogies were mobilised.[20]

The prototypal "winged souls" of the Neoplatonic "golden chain" (*chruse seira*) were Orpheus, Pythagoras and Plato. But already by the end of the fourth century AD, Porphyry, Iamblichus, Syrianus, Proclus and many others were regarded as divine. Garth Fowden has this to say:

> Likewise Hierokles described Ammonios as "divinely possessed (*enthousiasas*) with longing for the true goal of philosophy". Reflection on theological and philosophical truths was

---

19. Polymnia Athanassiadi, "Persecution and Response in Late Paganism: The Evidence of Damascius," in *The Journal of Hellenic Studies*, vol. CXIII, 1993, p. 6.

20. *Ibid.*, p. 5.

indeed widely accepted as a prerequisite of divinisation. Proclus . . . asserts that immersion in the mysteries of Platonic philosophy could result in divine possession, like a "Dionysiac frenzy"; and Olympiodorus listed four Platonic dialogues (*Timaeus, Respublica, Phaedrus, Theaetetus*) which in his opinion illustrated these *Platonikoi enthousiasmoi*.[21]

According to this tradition (*paradosis*), Plato himself received the complete science of the gods from Pythagorean and Orphic writings. The science of dialectic advocated by Plato is not found in the Orphico-Pythagorean theology, but both Orphism and Pythagoreanism (whatever these ambivalent terms may mean for different audiences) are viewed as being based on the ancient Egyptian and Babylonian revelations. The divine Plato only gave it scientific form, combining "the revelatory style of Pythagoreanism with the demonstrative method of Socrates".[22]

Hence, in this respect Socrates' approach is demonstrative (*apodeiktikon*) rather than revelatory. Now Syrianus, the spiritual guide of both Hermeias and Proclus, not only proclaimed the harmony (*sumphonia*) between Orpheus, Pythagoras and Plato, but also depicted Socrates as a kind of saviour—the divine avatar sent down to the world of becoming in order to bring the fallen souls back to the divine banquet (Hermeias, *In Phaedr.* I.1-5). This soteriological function of Socrates is modelled on the analogous function of Orpheus, though the initial meaning of the term *soteria* is related to the realm of public sponsorship, social benefits and graces provided by local patrons and divinized heroes. In the Hellenistic Greek world, any benefactor (*euergetes*) may be recognized and honoured as a saviour (*soter*).[23]

---

21. Garth Fowden, "The Pagan Holy Man in Late Antique Society," in *The Journal of Hellenic Studies*, vol. CII, 1982, p. 35.

22. Dominic J. O'Meara, *Pythagoras Revived: Mathematics and Philosophy in Late Antiquity* (Oxford: Clarendon Press, 1997), p. 148.

23. G.W. Bowersock, "The Imperial Cult: Perceptions and Persistence," in *Jewish and Christian Self-Definition, Vol.3: Self-Definition in the Graeco-*

However, in a metaphysical sense, the ability to save—the soul's immortalization or alleged "homecoming"—is the function and privilege of the benevolent gods. For example, the Chaldean Hekate as the "life-giving womb" and "lightning-receiving womb" (or as a formless fire, *aneideon pur*, visible throughout the cosmos) is indispensable for those seeking salvation: "Soteriologically minded philosophers and theurgists, who wished to assure the rising of their own souls, later advanced the idea that Hekate, by controlling the crossing of the boundary between humanity and divinity, either could aid the ascent or could force the descent of the soul."[24]

The divine-like souls of true philosophers are not entirely cut off from participation in contemplation of the Ideas. In a certain metaphorical sense, they still follow the heavenly retinue depicted in Plato's *Phaedrus*. They are "companions of the gods" (*opadous theon andras*), like the idealized and mythologized Socrates of Syrianus and Proclus. In short, Socrates is understood as an instrument of divine will. His system of pedagogy presumably belongs to the soteriological "golden chain" of Homer and Orpheus, and his philosophy is no less than a divinely inspired beneficial madness.

Both Orpheus and Socrates are presented as spiritual guides, that is, as inspired mystagogues able to reveal the ultimate vision of the Ideas, a vision regarded as initiation into the highest mysteries. Before starting his interpretation of the *Phaedrus* myth, Proclus explains: "These things are said by Socrates in the *Phaedrus* when he is clearly inspired (*enthousiazon*) and dealing with mystic matters" (*Plat. Theol.* IV.5, 18.23-25). And the citharist Orpheus, like Chiron the Centaur, half-brother of Zeus, "in a certain way embodies the mythical guide of souls most purely", as Ilsetraut Hadot says,

---

Roman World, ed. Ben F. Mayer and E.P. Sanders (London: SCM Press, 1982), p. 171.

24. Sarah Iles Johnston, *Hekate Soteira: A Study of Hekate's Roles in the Chaldean Oracles and Related Literature* (Atlanta: Scholars Press, 1990), p. 38.

"preparing a direct and material correspondence between music and wisdom."[25]

But philosophy is the highest art and highest music, as Plato's Socrates himself acknowledges (*Phaed.* 61a). Consequently, the exemplary poets and singers are *entheoi*, inspired ones, although feebly translated as "inspired", the Greek word *entheos* loses its literal force, according to Vlastos.[26] And Socrates is god-possessed (*katechomenos*); even more: "I am a seer (*mantis*)," he says (*Phaedr.* 242c), since the Greek term *mantis* may be rendered as "diviner" or "prophet". In a sense it is "god himself (*ho theos autos*) who speaks to us through them" (*Ion.* 234.d.3-4), since the possessed speakers "know nothing of the things they speak".

The Greek *entheos* literally means "within is a god" or "in god". This indwelling *theos* (not unlike the Egyptian *ba* in its simulated sacred receptacle) speaks from the person (or from the animated cultic statue) in a strange voice, sometimes resembling the so-called "language of the birds" or the primordial noise of the creative sound. The most common Greek terms for this or similar states are *mania* (madness, frenzy, inspiration) and *ekstasis* (to stand [or be] outside oneself). Every seer, filled by the ritually ignited and conventionally performed frenzy, stands in a special relationship to the deity, because the words he utters presuppose either the telestic madness of Dionysus, or the prophetic madness of Apollo.

But what about knowledge which is not human in its origin? Strictly speaking, this knowledge presupposes that the speaker himself knows nothing. According to Vlastos:

> In Socrates' view the effect of the god's entry into the poet is to drive out the poet's mind: when the god is in him the poet is "out of his mind", *ekphron*, or "intelligence is no longer

---

25. Ilsetraut Hadot, "The Spiritual Guide," in *Classical Mediterranean Spirituality: Egyptian, Greek, Roman*, ed. A.H. Armstrong (London: Routledge & Kegan Paul, 1986), p. 440.
26. Gregory Vlastos, *Socratic Piety*, p. 549.

present in him"; so he may find himself saying many things
which are admirable (*polla kai kala*) and true without knowing
what he is saying . . . it is because he is like the diviner that
the inspired poet is "out of his mind". . . . For Socrates, di-
viners, seers, oracle-givers and poets are all in the same boat.
All of them in his view are know-nothings, or rather, worse:
unaware of their sorry epistemic state, they set themselves up
as repositories of wisdom emanating from a divine, all-wise
source. What they say may be true; but even when it is true,
they are in no position to discern what there is in it that is
true.[27]

They convey truth to the extent that they repeat the divine
voice which may serve as a truth-speaking *kathegemon*, the one
who leads and who shows the way, and may deceive as Agam-
emnon allegedly was deceived by Zeus, although Proclus is
eager to explain this deception *kata ten aporrheton theorian*,
that is, according to the esoteric (or secret, unspoken, mysterious) mode of seeing. This is so, because the revealed myths
and hieratic customs may be "educational" (*paideutikoi*), or
appropriate for the young, and "more divinely inspired" (*en-
theastikoteroi*), that is, "more philosophical" (*philosophoteroi*)
and appropriate for the initiates (Proclus, *In Remp.* I.79.5-
18). As Robert Lamberton points out:

> When Proclus discusses the differences between Homer and
> Plato, he presents Homer as "inspired" and "ecstatic", an
> author who offers a direct revelation and is in contact with
> absolute truth. Plato is seen as coming later to the same in-
> formation and treating it differently, "establishing it solidly
> by the irrefutable methods of systematic thought" [*In Remp.*
> I.171-172].[28]

---

27. *Ibid.*, pp. 550 & 551.
28. Robert Lamberton, *Homer the Theologian: Neoplatonist Allegorical Reading and the Growth of the Epic Tradition*, (Berkeley: University of California Press, 1986), p. 194.

The Greek word for god (*theos*) is itself related to the act of the seer. The divine revelation may be received in the form of myth (*muthos*). Such a myth is to be used properly, because its surface is only a "veil" or "screen" (*parapetasma*), behind which another, metaphysical truth lies awaiting its inspired *hermeneus*. Even Homer's blindness is regarded as a divinely established symbol that points to the dark and transcendental character of Homer's vision. In this respect, Proclus argues that Socrates (the literary personage of Plato's *Republic*), in fact, is deceived regarding "the way in which myths represent the truth".[29]

So what does it mean to be a seer—both the teller of myths and the inspired interpreter of the revealed myth? As Walter Burkert explains the Greek terms:

> . . . an interpreted sign is *thesphaton*, the seer is *theoprotos*, and what he does is a *theiazein* or *entheazein*. . . . Insofar as the seer speaks in an abnormal state, he requires in turn someone who formulates his utterances, the *prophetes*. The word for seer itself, *mantis*, is connected with the Indo-European root for mental power, and is also related to *mania*, madness.[30]

Be that as it may, the Platonic philosophy is viewed by Proclus as divine philosophy, because it "shone forth" (*eklampsai*) for the first time "through the good grace of the gods".[31] Therefore, its amazing noetic tradition repeats the dazzling appearance of Phanes, the Orphic Atum, whose primaeval "shining forth" from the ineffable darkness constitutes the noetic pleroma, the mound of Heliopolis. Accordingly, the ineffable Night is the Egg from which the solar bird sprang forth on the first morning—*in illo tempore*.

---

29. *Ibid.*, p. 196.

30. Walter Burkert, *Greek Religion*, tr. John Raffan (Cambridge, MA: Harvard University Press, 2000), p. 112.

31. John Glucker, *Antiochus and the Late Academy* (Göttingen: Vandenhoeck and Ruprecht, 1978), p. 312.

IV

Proclus presents Socrates' "celebration" of the realm beyond the heavens (*huperouranios topos*) as a "symbolic description" (*sumbolike apangelia*). He says that "the mode which aims to speak of the divine by means of symbols is Orphic and generally appropriate to those who write about divine myths" (*Plat. Theol.* I.4.10.6ff). Consequently, the myth narrated in Plato's *Phaedrus* is taken "to be not only inspired but also telestic, which for him means theurgic".[32]

Hence, Proclus interprets the images and events of the Phaedrus myth in terms of theurgy, arguing that the realm beyond the heavens where the Ideas are to be contemplated corresponds to the three Orphic Nights. Anne Sheppard considers that Syrianus, the spiritual guide of Proclus, "did not distinguish between the inspired, theurgic mode of discourse on the one hand and the symbolic, Orphic mode on the other".[33] Even for Proclus (in spite of his advanced technical terminology), the prophetic madness, philosophical frenzy, theurgic rites and their allegorical or symbolic interpretation constitute a single metaphysical set of references related to the way in which the soul ascends to the noetic realm, whence it may be reunited with the highest reality.

In relation to this exposition of the Orphic and Platonic aids to recollection, "which form a continual initiation into the perfect mystic vision" (*Phaedr.* 249c), one may wonder what it means to be possessed by a god, or to be a prophet in the wider context of ancient Egyptian and Mesopotamian cultures.

Arguing that the Greek verb *gignosko* (from which derives *gnosis*, knowledge) in early times is often combined with verbs of seeing (though "vision", in this case, may be understood as

---

32. Anne Sheppard, "Plato's Phaedrus in the Theologia Platonica," in *Proclus et la Théologie platonicienne*, ed. A. Ph. Segonds and C. Steel, (Leuven: University Press; Paris: Les Belles Lettres, 2000), p. 419.

33. *Ibid.*, p. 422.

an exceptional supra-normal faculty), J. Gonda attempts to place the oracular soothsayers and poets on the same footing as prophets and philosophers.[34] In Greece, the specific sanctuary or holy place where the gods are thought to be present and may offer counsel is called *chresterion* or *manteion*, and rendered as *oraculum* by the Romans. In these places, like in the Syrian and Mesopotamian temples, the god speaks directly from a priest or a prophet who enters the state of possession (*enthousiasmos*).

Hence, a prophet, as an inspired seer, somewhat emptied of himself and "filled with the god" (being a possessed *enthousiastes*), is a representative of the speaking deity. Even if this attribution is sometimes just a literary convention turned into a compelling promise of an act of salvation, the magic power was thought to be inherent in the mighty word of any successful demagogue. Whether or not we would like to describe this mythically determined oracular performer and possessed speaker as an inspired public teacher or as a prophet (the Greek *prophetes* who relates cult legends at festivals),[35] the prophecy itself may be defined as a perpetual confirmation of particular cosmological, epistemological and socio-political principles sustained through a ritually performed exegesis. Even the ancient Hebrew "prophet" (*nabi*), in its initial context, may appear simply "as a courier for an important letter passed between two politically interested parties, perhaps co-conspirators of some sort".[36]

---

34. J. Gonda, *The Vision of the Vedic Poets* (New Delhi: Munshiram Manoharlal Publishers, 1984), pp. 24 & 14.

35. *Ibid.*, p. 14.

36. Joel Sweek, "Inquiring for the State in the Ancient Near East: Delineating Political Location," in *Magic and Divination in the Ancient World*, ed. Leda Ciraolo and Jonathan Seidel (Leiden: Brill/Styx, 2002), p. 55.

V

What, then, is prophecy? The use of this very concept is controversial, mainly due to a Judaeo-Christian theological bias and the related "romantic perception of the biblical prophets as tormented individuals of great literary talent".[37]

The almost unquestioned dogma of prophetic revelation as an epistemological category embodied in the book is a scribal construct of Mesopotamian origin. The post-exilic religious bureaucrats of Second Temple Judaism decided that the only way in which the divine Patron can speak to His vassals (the Israelites as His contractual slaves and warriors) was through the written text. Karel van der Toorn discusses the rhetoric of prophetic revelation in connection with the legitimizing construction of the prophetic experience, with the increasing emphasis on writing as the primary and privileged vehicle of prophecy. He writes:

> When prophecy became primarily a literary genre, the prophets were posthumously transformed into authors. . . . When the Hebrew scribes adopted the revelation paradigm in connection with the prophetic literature, they took the vision (*hazon*) to be the classic mode of prophetic revelation. That is why the rubrics of the prophetic books often use the terminology of the visionary experience as the technical vocabulary for prophecy, even for prophets whose oracles do not refer to any vision. . . . The novelty of the scribal construct of prophecy as a revelation lies in the reference to written texts. The scribes developed the notion of the prophet as a scribe, and of his message as a secret revealed by heavenly figures, to legitimize the fact that the prophets had become books.[38]

---

37. Karel van der Toorn, *Scribal Culture and the Making of the Hebrew Bible* (Cambridge, MA: Harvard University Press, 2009), p. 190.
38. *Ibid.*, pp. 231 & 232.

In this case, God (the mighty Patron of the chosen zealots) is presented as speaking only through the written text, itself now attached to the prestigious *taklimtu* category of Babylonian writings. The Akkadian word *taklimtu* (literally meaning "demonstration") stands for "revelation" and "preserves a reminiscence of the time in which revelation was primarily thought of as a visual experience".[39] The premise of the Babylonian cuneiform literature is that, unless revealed, wisdom (*nemequ*) remains hidden, thus constituting a conception of esoteric knowledge and interest in the "broad understanding" (*uznu rapashtu*) and "profound wisdom" (*hasisu palku*) of the Deep, attributed to the *apkallu* sages, which assisted the emergence of the revelation paradigm; a paradigm that asserted the authority of the written tradition perpetuated by the learned expert (*ummanu mudu*) who guarded the secret lore of the great gods (*ummanu mudu nasir pirishti ili rabuti*).[40]

Scribal wisdom itself (along with the broad comprehension of "secret things") is god-given. The privileged texts "from the mouth of Ea" (*sha pi Ea*) may be witnessed as "the writings of Ea" (*shitru sha Ea*). It was held that Ea dictated his revelations to Adepa, the legendary *apkallu* sage, one of the "seven brilliant *apkallus, puradu*-fish of the sea".[41] Oannes-Adapa transmitted this wisdom of Ea (*nemeq Ea*) through the subsequent written tradition. Adapa's patron Ea is called *bel nemeqi*, the Lord of Wisdom. The exceptional value of his wisdom is recognized by the sixteenth century BC text on behalf of the early Kassite ruler: "May Ea, the god of the depths, grant him perfect wisdom" (*Ea bel naghim nemeqam lishklilshu*).[42]

---

39. *Ibid.*, p. 212.

40. Ronald F.G. Sweet, "The Sage in Akkadian Literature: A Philological Study," in *The Sage in Israel and the Ancient Near East*, ed. John G. Gammie and Leo G. Perdue (Winona Lake, IN: Eisenbrauns, 1990), p. 60.

41. Shlomo Izre'el, *Adapa and the South Wind: Language Has the Power of Life and Death* (Winona Lake, IN: Eisenbrauns, 2001), p. 4.

42. Ronald F.G. Sweet, *ibid.*, p. 52.

Similarly, Marduk provides deep understanding (*uznu*) and intelligence (*hasisu*), and Nabu, the heavenly Scribe who knows everything, brings forth wise teachings (*ihzi nemeqi*). Van der Toorn describes the situation when the written tradition of the Mesopotamian scribes supplanted the oral tradition and, as a consequence, faced the problem of legitimacy and authority. He writes:

> The scribes found their new source of authority in the concept of divine revelation. Through the construct of an antediluvian revelation from Ea to the *apkallus*, transmitted in an unbroken chain of sages, scribes, and scholars, the written tradition could claim a legitimacy issuing from the gods. In support of the theory that the revelation paradigm was an answer to a legitimacy problem, one can point to the emergence of the rhetoric of secrecy. At about the same time that the Mesopotamian scribes and scholars began to speak of the tradition as having been revealed, they started to emphasize its secret nature.[43]

VI

And so, what about the prophets themselves? Are they "prophets" in the sense of seers—the beholders of divine epiphanies at festivals with their splendid processions, portable divine images and barques? Let us remember that the Greek word *theoria* initially meant contemplation of the gods at their festivals, before it started to mean the beholding of the well-ordered Pythagorean cosmos or the Platonic Ideas. Are the prophets "messengers" in the sense of heralds, announcers, ceremonial declaimers in the manner of reciters who perform the traditional poems and myths at the annual festivals? Or

---

43. Karel van der Toorn, *Scribal Culture and the Making of the Hebrew Bible*, p. 219.

are they the professional actors on the stage of the Dionysiac theatre?

Modern Western convention tends to emphasize the "inner experience", "spontaneous inspiration", and the "moral educational" pedigree of the imagined "prophetic" human-divine communication, though this kind of theologically asserted communication may be simply a matter of cultural definition and classification. The proposed taxonomy engages a division of social and metaphysical roles that may be performed.

There is no single equivalent of the Greek words "prophet" (*prophetes*) and "prophecy" (*propheteia*) in the ancient Near Eastern languages. In addition, the word "prophecy" is liable to a certain semantic confusion, since it is commonly equated with foretelling the future. Nevertheless, prophecy may be defined as a process of communication—not unlike a well-organized royal "postal service", prominent in the Achaemenid Persian empire, when the conception of angelic messengers started to emerge. According to Martti Nissinen, this consisted of the divine sender of the message, the message (classified as "revelation") itself, the transmitter of the message (the prophet as postal officer and courier), and the recipient of the message, usually the king.[44] Nissinen comments:

> The Mesopotamian sources include two distinguishable types of texts, both of which have been characterized as "prophecy": 1) the verbal messages, allegedly sent by a deity and transmitted by a human intermediary to the addressee, and 2) the "Akkadian Prophecies", also called "apocalypses", which predict historical events, mostly *ex eventu*.[45]

In a sense, the prophet is the mouthpiece of a deity when the message to be transmitted is not initially a "written document" (or a material cuneiform tablet brought from the divine

---

44. Martti Nissinen, *References to Prophecy in Neo-Assyrian Sources* (Helsinki: The Neo-Assyrian Text Corpus Project, 1998), p. 6.
45. *Ibid.*, p. 7.

counsel), but an oral command, advice or reproach, later presented to the addressee in the written form of a manifesto-like dispatch. When reference is made to the spoken word (*abutu, dibbu*) of a deity in the Neo-Assyrian sources, the speaking deity is either Ishtar or Mallissu, the main goddess of prophecy.[46]

Among the words which imply prophetic activity, two are important: *mahhu*, derived from *mahu*, "to be in a frenzy, to become mad", and *raggimu*, derived from *ragamu*, "to shout, to proclaim". Consequently, the Assyrian *raggimu* is the "pronouncer" or "speaker", and the *muhhum* is a type of madman, like the Hebrew *meshugga*, "a term occasionally used as a synonym for *nabi*".[47]

All these terms may be used as synonyms and contrasted to the *baru*—the reader of the divine script of the cosmos and interpreter of the signs inscribed on the livers of sacrificial animals. The *baru* (haruspex) is viewed as belonging to the "golden chain" of transmission beginning with the Sumerian king Enmeduranki, the ultimate prototype of the Hebrew Enoch. Enmeduranki, the ruler of Sippar, was brought to the assembly (*puhru*) of the gods by Shamash and Adad. There he was seated on a golden throne and the divine secrets were revealed to him. The gods gave (*iddinu*) him the tablet of the gods (*tuppi ilani*, that is, the "divine book") which contained the "secret science". As Helge Kvanvig points out: "The tablet emphasizes the esoteric character of the divine wisdom revealed to Enmeduranki."[48]

The Assyrian prophecies are inseparable from the royal ideology, since the Neo-Assyrian Empire and the "kingdom of heaven" are interconnected through the power of Ishtar, represented by the sacred tree. The cult of Ishtar (the goddess herself viewed as the "breath" of Ashur, analogous to the later

---

46. *Ibid.*, p. 10.
47. Abraham Malamat, *Mari and the Bible* (Leiden: Brill, 1998), p. 66.
48. Helge S. Kvanvig, *Roots of Apocalyptic: The Mesopotamian Background of the Enoch Figure and of the Son of Man* (Neukirchen-Vluyn: Neukirchener Verlag), 1988, p. 188.

Gnostic Sophia) constitutes the Assyrian esoteric doctrine of salvation. In the universalized imperial context, prophecy, mysticism and royal ideology are inseparable. Gilgamesh is the prototype of the perfect Assyrian king, and Ishtar is the divine mother who gives birth to him. No wonder, then, that one of the Assyrian prophetesses (*ragintu*) "identifies herself with Gilgamesh roaming the desert in search of eternal life".[49] As Simo Parpola relates:

> For a spiritually pure person, union with God was believed to be possible not only in death but in life as well. This belief provides the doctrinal basis of Assyrian prophecy: when filled with divine spirit, the prophet not only becomes a seat for the Goddess but actually one with her, and thus can foresee future things. . . . The purpose of the act—which certainly was the culmination of a long process of spiritual preparation—was to turn the devotee into a living image of Ishtar: an androgynous person totally beyond the passions of flesh.[50]

Let us explore the following analogy: both the god-chosen Assyrian king and the devotee of Ishtar play the role of Ashur's son or of Mullissu's son. Likewise, the Neoplatonic mystic may seek to be integrated into the universal hypostasis of Hekate Soteira or Athena Soteira. Ishtar as "virgin of light" marks the presence of God (*Ashshur*, the only, universal God, viewed as "the totality of gods", *gabbu ilani Ashshur*).[51] At the same time, Ishtar is the word of God and the way of salvation. As a rule, the Assyrian prophets belong to the cultic community of Ishtar's devotees (*assinnu, nash pilaqqi*) and share their esoteric mystical lore concerning the ascent and salvation of the soul.[52]

---

49. Simo Parpola, *Assyrian Prophecies* (Helsinki: Helsinki University Press, the Neo-Assyrian Text Corpus Project, 1997), p. L.
50. *Ibid.*, p. XXXIV.
51. *Ibid.*, pp. XXI & LXXXI.
52. *Ibid.*, p. XLVII.

Similarly, theurgic divination in Neoplatonism may be regarded as a means of ascent and unification—"standing outside" of one's normal state of consciousness, that is, in *ecstasis* and frenzy. This entails an all-consuming presence of the divine as the inspired theurgist is seized by the invading god. This divine invasion may be equated to the active irruption of the dazzling noetic light within the purified recipient, or rather, in his mirror-like *phantasia*. Emma Clarke explains the matter as follows:

> Iamblichus argues that the imagination is manipulated by the gods and receives divine *phantasmata* during inspiration. He consistently describes god-sent visions as *phantasmata* or *phantasiai*. . . . Porphyry writes that people themselves "imagine" (*phantazontai*) or "are divinely inspired according to their imaginative faculty" (*kata to phantastikon theiazousin*), whereas Iamblichus insists that the imagination is affected from the outside—divine power "illuminates with a divine light the aetherial and luciform vehicle surrounding the soul, from which divine visions occupy the imaginative faculty in us, driven by the will of the gods. . . . " An inspired individual is not thinking or using his imagination—his imagination is being made use of by the gods. Left to its own devices, untouched by the gods, the imagination produces mere (human) phantasms which have no place in the process of inspiration. . . . The imagination is therefore valued only as a passive receptacle of divine visions.[53]

VII

The prophetic messages attributed to the accredited Babylonian prophets, including those who served in various temples and those perceived as madmen, Abraham Malamat relates

---

53. Emma C. Clarke, *Iamblichus' De Mysteriis: A Manifesto of the Miraculous* (Aldershot: Ashgate, 2001), pp. 84 & 85.

to the category of "intuitive prophecy".[54] Since the so-called "scientific" Akkadian divination practised by the *barum* is described as both typical and rational, the "intuitive divination" attested at Mari seems to be both atypical and irrational.[55] But this observation is not entirely correct. In certain cases, prophecy may be described in terms of ceremonial rhetoric— the human calls and divine answers which demand the taking of important political decisions. To categorize this conventional dialectical play as "intuitive" means to be under the spell of an exalted Western romanticism. This influential theory of aesthetics invents and cherishes the "spontaneous inner experiences" of exceptional individuals, deliberately forgetting the ritualized literary background of such "spontaneous" social concerns.

The Neo-Assyrian and Mari texts, however, present the local prophets (*apilum, muhhum, nabum, raggimu*) as those who receive divine messages involuntarily: the messages are not regarded as invented or created by the *muhhum*. Lester Grabbe states: "When prophets speak openly in a temple, this looks like spontaneous spirit possession: the spirit comes upon them, and they become a mouthpiece for the deity."[56]

Or do they believe this is so and need this belief literally as it stands, along with the "ecstatic testimony" and the subsequent "theatrical performance"? The stereotypical language of this seemingly spontaneous play amounts to a strategically managed language which functions as the hermeneutic of the myth, as the reconfirmation of the temple tradition, of its socio-economic premises, expectations, hopes and dreams. As a rule, the contemporary cosmic geography and its pecu-

---

54. Abraham Malamat, *Mari and the Bible*, pp. 59-82. (Ch. 6: "Intuitive Prophecy – A General Survey," originally published in: A. Malamat, Mari and the Early Israelite Experience, 1992, pp. 79-86).

55. Ibid., p. 60.

56. Lester L. Grabbe, "Ancient Near Eastern Prophecy from an Anthropological Perspective," in *Prophecy in its Ancient Near Eastern Context: Mesopotamian, Biblical, and Arabian Perspectives*, ed. Martti Nissinen (Atlanta: Society of Biblical Literature, 2000), p. 18.

liarities are involved. Therefore, "it is often difficult to distinguish between actual prophetic oracles and literary prophecies created by scribes."[57] No wonder the prophets themselves
are sometimes viewed as scribes whose speeches or reports
are not performed in public as the standards of the sacred
"revelatory theatre" and of epic consciousness would require.
Instead, they are composed as oracular collections and royal
inscriptions.[58]

In the Mesopotamian city of Mari (eighteenth century BC)
the mediators between the heavenly divine assembly (*puhru*)
and the earthly royal court bear the titles of *apilum/apiltum*
("answerers"), *muhhum/muhhutum* ("ecstatics"), *assinnum*
("cult singers"), and *nabum* ("ones called"). The messages
they bring from the gods (Dagan, Addu of Halab, Shamash,
Marduk, Nergal) and the goddesses (Annunitum, Diritum,
Hishametum, Ninhursgga, Ishtar) are taken seriously by the
political authorities, although these prophetic messages are
subordinated to other means of divine communication.[59]

Accordingly, the identity of the prophet cannot be taken
as a guarantee for the validity and truth of the prophecy pro-
nounced, or "shouted" (*ragamu*), presumably in a state of real
or solemnly feigned frenzy. But a possession cult *par excellence*
and the related professionalization of prophecy pertain to the
domain and supervision of Ishtar. Van der Toorn writes:

> Ishtar was deemed capable to produce, by way of ecstasy, a
> metamorphosis in her worshipers. Men might be turned into
> women, and women were made to behave as men. . . . There is

---

57. *Ibid.*, p. 25.

58. David L. Petersen, "Defining Prophecy and Prophetic Literature,"
in *Prophecy in its Ancient Near Eastern Context: Mesopotamian, Biblical, and
Arabian Perspectives*, ed. Martti Nissinen (Atlanta: Society of Biblical
Literature, 2000), p. 42.

59. Herbert B. Huffmon, "A Company of Prophets: Mari, Assyria,
Israel," in *Prophecy in its Ancient Near Eastern Context: Mesopotamian, Biblical,
and Arabian Perspectives*, ed. Martti Nissinen (Atlanta: Society of Biblical
Literature, 2000), p. 49.

evidence that at least some of the Neo-Assyrian prophetesses were in reality men, or rather self-castrated transvestites. Their outward appearance was interpreted as a display of Ishtar's transforming powers. Possessed by the divine, they were the obvious persons to become mouthpieces of the gods.[60]

Their prophetic utterances were not metaphysical slogans or theological *shahadas*, as the modern esoteric dreamer would tend to imagine, but the utterances of a deity, revealed while standing in the temple before the animated hieratic statue. In the name of a particular god an oracle is delivered by the temple servant, or rather the deity (Dagan, for instance) opens the mouth of and speaks from within his image. Van der Toorn comments on this rite as follows:

The Old Babylonian gods grant prophetic revelations only in the sanctuary. Dreams may occur at other places, but prophecy, properly speaking, is confined to the temple. . . . When a god speaks directly through the mouth of a prophet, the latter utters the prophecy first in the temple. The prophet (*apilum* or *apiltum*) "rises" (*itbi*) or "stands" (*izziz*) to deliver the divine message in the temple. The ecstatic (*muhhum*), too, receives the revelation in a sanctuary; this is the place where he or she gets into a frenzy (*immahi, immahu*), utters loud cries (*shitassu*), and gives the oracle. When a prophet delivers an oracle outside the sanctuary, at the residence of the royal deputy for instance, he repeats an oracle revealed to him in the sanctuary. For that reason the prophet presents himself as a messenger of the god (DN *ishpuranni*): he transmits the message (*temum*), which he receives at an earlier stage.[61]

---

60. Karel van der Toorn, "Mesopotamian Prophecy between Immanence and Transcendence: A Comparison of Old Babylonian and Neo-Assyrian Prophecy," in *Prophecy in its Ancient Near Eastern Context: Mesopotamian, Biblical, and Arabian Perspectives*, ed. Martti Nissinen (Atlanta: Society of Biblical Literature, 2000), p. 79.
61. *Ibid.*, p. 80.

This means that the "house of god" is the most suitable place for these continuing encounters with the divine and the forthcoming revelations. And revelation itself is to a certain extent the standard cultic procedure in the "audience hall" of the Lord. It is performed in the divine palace (since the temple is a deity's household and palace) whose ceremonial patterns follow the established framework of the private and official life of the royalty (although, metaphysically speaking, the opposite is true).

Therefore, in accordance with the rules of cultic etiquette, the prophet is positioned in front of the hieratic statue as the servant or herald stands before the king. He stands—or rather lies in prostration—and listens. The Mesopotamian hieratic statue—that of the enthroned deity in full regalia, seated in the holy of holies—is not a religious picture, but an icon imbued with a god's essential powers and endowed with divine radiance. The divine form (*bunnannu*) or image (*salam, salmu*) is not manufactured by human artists, whose hands are symbolically cut off with a tamarisk sword, but ritually conceived by the gods themselves and born in a special workshop, the *bit mummi*.[62] Yet a clear distinction is maintained between the god and his statue,[63] which serves as a means to make the deity visible on earth.

In this respect, the entire temple complex functions, metaphorically speaking, like a "nuclear power station" that provides all material and spiritual sustenance for the surrounding land and its inhabitants, viewed respectively as a deity's private fief and vassals. The animated image is presumed able to perceive what happens in the earthly realm, to reign over the kingdom, communicate through the court messengers

---

62. Victor Avigdor Hurowitz, *The Mesopotamian God Image, From Womb to Tomb*, Journal of the American Oriental Society 123, 1, 2003, p. 153.

63. Michael B. Dick, "Prophetic Parodies of Making the Cult Image," in *Born in Heaven, Made on Earth: The Making of the Cult Image in the Ancient Near East*, ed. Michael B. Dick (Winona Lake, IN: Eisenbrauns, 1999), p. 33.

(apostles) and consume victuals. The mouth washing ritual activates the statue's noetic and perceptive functions, as Angelika Berlejung remarks: "The ritual thus enabled it to become the pure epiphany of its god and to be a fully interacting and communicating partner for the king, the priests and the faithful."[64]

When the prophet speaks in the name of a god in the temple, he makes himself an extension of the god whose holy face he contemplates. When he has this privilege, neither is the statue's face veiled, nor the statue itself hidden behind a screen.[65] In a parallel fashion, the divine Pythagoras used to speak from behind a curtain, thus imitating the oracular statue. It is, therefore, no surprise that Pythagoras "imitated the Orphic mode of writing"[66] and his disciples looked upon all his utterances as the oracles of God.[67]

This encounter with the divine statue (veiled or otherwise) is the ultimate paradigm for mystical longing, contemplation and union by means of liturgical communications, including sound, smell and vision. To Plato's "madness" corresponds the Orphic "frenzy" (*oistros*), as Peter Kingsley observes;[68] and, we might add, to the Orphic frenzy corresponds the Mesopotamian prophetic madness (entering into a trance, *immahu*), experienced in the form of ecstasy before the *salmu*.

The cultic scenario of prophetic frenzy apparently explains why traditional skills of divination should be related to this soul-transforming, illuminating and elevating standing in the

---

64. Angelika Berlejung, "Washing the Mouth: The Consecration of Divine Images in Mesopotamia," in *The Image and the Book: Iconic Cults, Aniconism, and the Rise of Book Religion in Israel and the Ancient Near East*, ed. Karel van der Toorn (Leuven: Uitgeverij Peeters, 1997), p. 72.

65. *The Pythagorean Sourcebook and Library: An Anthology of Ancient Writings Which Relate to Pythagoras and Pythagorean Philosophy*, compiled and translated by Kenneth Sylvan Guthrie, ed. David R. Fideler (Grand Rapids: Phanes Press, 1987), p. 74 (Iamblichus, *Vit. Pyth.* 17).

66. *Ibid.*, p. 95 (Iamblichus, *Vit. Pyth.* 28).

67. *Ibid.*, p. 145 (Diogenes Laertius, *The Life of Pythagoras*).

68. Peter Kingsley, *Ancient Philosophy, Mystery, and Magic: Empedocles and Pythagorean Tradition* (Oxford: Clarendon Press, 1995), pp. 261-62.

place where the divine presence is manifested. For Iamblichus, the Syrian Neoplatonist, divination (*mantike*) and theurgic ascension (*anagoge*) coincide. He argues: "Only divine
mantic prediction (*he theia mantike*), therefore, conjoined with
the gods, truly imparts to us a share in divine life, partaking
as it does in the foreknowledge and the intellections of the
gods, and renders us, in truth, divine" (*De myster*. 289.3-5).[69]

Hence, the "emptied" prophet is the theurgic receptacle
filled with the divine light and life emanating from the seeing
and speaking deity. This real or imagined theophany implies
the prophet's annihilation (in the sense of the Sufi *fana*) and
God's exaltation. As Van der Toorn observes:

> There is no room for misunderstanding as to who is speaking.
> That is why we never find, in any of the reports describing
> a prophecy delivered in the temple, a phrase identifying the
> divine speaker. . . . The only time the prophet finds it neces-
> sary to say that god so-and-so has sent him (DN *ishpuranni*)
> is when the prophecy is transmitted to someone outside the
> sanctuary.[70]

Eventually, the Neo-Assyrian prophets themselves became
like interiorized and portable sanctuaries, and not bound to
the presence of the material divine image in order to establish contact with the gods. Although images and statues were
their cultic receptacles and symbolic bodies, these gods at the
same time permanently resided in heaven, and consequently,
they could also be praised inwardly, within the human body-
temple. Hence, a message from the god or a revelation may
occur outside the sanctuary. In late antiquity, a similar at-
titude became prominent among the Neoplatonists, namely,

69. *Iamblichus De mysteriis*, tr. Emma C. Clarke, John M. Dillon and
Jackson P. Hershbell (Atlanta: Society of Biblical Literature, 2003), p. 347.

70. Karel van der Toorn, *Mesopotamian Prophecy between Immanence and
Transcendence: A Comparison of Old Babylonian and Neo-Assyrian Prophecy*, p.
82.

that "the prophetic spirit cannot be confined to one place only, but is present in the whole cosmos being co-extensive with God."[71]

However, sometimes it seems that only the "professional madmen" can receive such messages and afterwards come to the aid of the king to whom all prophecies within the empire presumably are addressed, or at least indirectly concern. These prophecies promise the intervention of the gods and their mighty support from heaven. As Van der Toorn remarks:

> Whereas the Old Babylonian gods secure the success of the king by their presence on earth, as auxiliaries of his army, the Neo-Assyrian deities influence the outcome of political and military conflict by an intervention from heaven. In the Old Babylonian prophecies, the battle in which the gods become involved remains within the human horizon; in the Neo-Assyrian texts, however, the battle takes on cosmic dimensions.[72]

VIII

Let us turn briefly to the Egyptian priestly titles and their functions. In Late Period Egypt, it seems that the rules of purity were imposed upon the population at large, and not only the serving priests and ascetics. Therefore, the Romanized Hermetic description of Egypt as the *templum totius mundi*— the temple of the whole world—is to a certain extent justified.

Cultic purification is a necessary condition for entering the house of the god (*hut-neter*), located in the centre of the divine household (*per-neter*), and becoming the god's prophet—the royal deputy and "deified" performer of sacramental union. In the temple liturgy, the name of the deity is uttered

---

71. Polymnia Athanassiadi, "Philosophers and Oracles: Shifts of Authority in Late Paganism," *Byzantion: Revue internationale des Etudes byzantines*, Bruxelles, LXII, 1992, p. 58
72. Karel van der Toorn, *ibid.*, p. 84.

loudly and then followed by the self-presentation of the entering priest.

The purified priests play the role of both the king and the gods themselves, thus the temple liturgy is turned into a type of theurgy. But neither the priests nor the animated cult images are the gods as they are in their transcendent metaphysical realm. Rather, they serve as vehicles for the divine irradiation, communication and contextual presence: "In the temple liturgy the self-presentation consists mainly of affirmations of the type 'I am the god such and such,' usually a divine intermediary such as Thot, Shu, Horus, but also Isis and Nephtys, occasionally preceded by the affirmation that the entering priest is indeed pure."[73]

The Egyptian priests are designated as *hemu-neter*, "servants of the god", like the servants of household staff.[74] As Ronald Williams remarks, the title *hemu-neter* was applied to a grade of temple priest, and was rendered by the Greek term *prophetes*, "the interpreter of the divine will".[75] More exactly, the higher priests of the Egyptian temple were divided into the categories of *hem-neter* (prophet) and *uab* (priest, the pure one). Consequently, the term *prophetes* denoted a certain particular liturgical function and also served as a designation of the higher priestly class (*hiereis*), itself divided into five subcategories.

According to John Gee, during the daily temple liturgy the officiant pronounces two statements of identity. While taking the incense burner, he says: "I am a priest and I am pure," and during the ritual of "undoing the white cloth", he says: "I am

73. Robert Meyer, "Magical Ascesis and Moral Purity in Ancient Egypt," in *Transformations of the Inner Self in Ancient Religions*, ed. Jan Assmann and Guy G. Stroumsa (Leiden: Brill, 1999), p. 59.

74. Jan Assmann, *The Search for God in Ancient Egypt*, tr. David Lorton (Ithaca and London: Cornell University Press, 2001), p. 29.

75. Ronald J. Williams, "The Sage in Egyptian Literature," in *The Sage in Israel and the Ancient Near East*, ed. John G. Gammie and Leo G. Perdue (Winona Lake, IN: Eisenbrauns, 1990), p. 26.

a prophet; it is the king who has commanded me to see the god."[76]

The title *hem-neter* is conventionally expressed in Greek as *prophetes*, and *uab* as *hiereus*. The statements *ink uab* (I am a priest) and *ink hem-neter* (I am a prophet) indicate the two main levels of the temple hierarchy. All priests belonged to the *uab* category because they were the "purified ones", but some of them were selected or appointed as the prophets—the spokesmen of the gods. As Christiane Zivie-Coche observes:

> The clergy of Amun had a "first prophet" who was at the summit of the hierarchy, as well as a second, third, and fourth prophet, each the sole holder of his rank, and then a mass of undifferentiated prophets. In principle, only the first prophet had access to the holy of holies, while the others, accompanied by lector-priests or ritualists, whose specialty was reading the papyrus rolls, stopped at the hall of offerings.[77]

All priests were simply officially appointed substitutes for the pharaoh, or rather, vehicles and instruments that reactivated his delegated powers, like the so-called *ushabty* figures which enabled the deceased Egyptian to participate in the obligatory liturgical work in the afterlife, instead of otherwise missing it. In this respect, the pharaoh is regarded as virtually the sole and omnipresent Priest of the state. He is the chief Mystagogue of his administrative apparatus and the singular Mystic, contemplating (in principle or in fact) the radiant face of his divine Patron-Father. And why? Because the pharaoh symbolizes and represents humanity as a whole: "The king is the sole terrestrial being qualified to communi-

76. John Gee, "Prophets, Initiation and the Egyptian Temple," *Journal of the Society for the Study of Egyptian Antiquities* 31, 2004, p. 97.

77. Francoise Dunand and Christiane Zivie-Coche, *Gods and Men in Egypt: 3000 BCE to 395 CE*, tr. David Lorton (Ithaca and London: Cornell University Press, 2004), p. 103.

cate with the gods because . . . the sacred communication cannot take place between a god and a merely human being, but only between god and god."[78]

The pharaoh, as the titulary son of Ra, is able to delegate his power of cultic communication to the temple staff. In such circumstances all constitutive elements of the telestic performance must be symbolic, since "everything in this sacred game becomes a kind of hieroglyph," according to Jan Assmann:

> It is in the role of the king that the priest is able to assume the role of a god. He plays the god because a cultic spell is divine utterance. The cultic scene, therefore, implies three levels of symbolization: 1) a priest confronting a statue; 2) the king confronting a god; 3) a god (whose role is played by the king represented by the priest) conversing with another god. . . . This tripartite system of religious symbolization is reminiscent of Greek mystery religions which are reported to imply the same three kinds of symbolic expression: 1) *dromenon* (what is to be done: action); 2) *deiknumenon* (what is to be shown: representation); 3) *legomenon* (what is to be said: language).[79]

To be initiated into royal service and be offered the status of cultic substitute for the son of Ra means to acquire

---

78. Jan Assmann, "Semiosis and Interpretation in Ancient Egyptian Ritual," in *Interpretation in Religion*, ed. Shlomo Biderman and Ben-Ami Scharfstein (Leiden: E.J. Brill, 1992), p. 92.

79. *Ibid.*, p. 94. The tripartite system, in the Egyptian case, has three modes of symbolic expression: 1) an action of the priest offering something; 2) pictoral representation of the pharaoh before the god on temple walls and in ritual papyri; 3) language (liturgical formulae and interpretations). According to Jan Assmann: "The temple reliefs of the Late period reflect a full-fledged tradition of ritual exegesis, a culture of interpretation . . . applied not to texts—as in the more-or-less contemporaneous Alexandrian and Jewish institutions of interpretation—but to pictures. However, this culture of interpretation is anything but a symptom of Hellenistic influence; on the contrary, it is deeply rooted in the Egyptian cult" (*ibid.*, p. 99).

the position and rank of prophet in the sense of the Graeco-Egyptian *prophetes*. Only by being initiated as the servant of god (*hem-neter*) can one enter into the temple as the "living servant of Ra" (*hem ankh en ra*) in order to see all forms of the god and all secret things.

The purpose of this initiation (*bes*) consists in seeing the deity, that is, in gazing at the image (*sekhem, tut*) of the god. The watcher (like the Platonic *theoros*) is to be united with the god's *ba* (manifestation, godlike radiance) in the tremendous contemplation of the divine truth and beauty.

Likewise in Neoplatonism, the dialectical and telestic becoming like the divine (*homoiosin*) leads to unification (*he arrhetos henosis*) with the god through the contemplation of his animated statue, for the telestic art makes the statues in the here below (*ta tede agalmata*) to be like the gods by means of symbols and mysterious theurgic tokens (*dia tinon sumbolon kai aporrheton sunthematon*: Proclus, *In Crat.* 51, p.19, 12ff).[80]

For Proclus, the true divine madness is to be equated with (or located in) the "one of the soul", the henadic summit of one's psychic and noetic topography by means of which the theurgist is united with the One.[81] Through the divine *maniai*—be it "prophetic madness according to Truth", "erotic madness according to Beauty", or "poetical madness according to divine Symmetry"—the philosopher's soul is linked to the gods, and "this form of life is that of the ultimate mystical experience of the ultimate unification."[82]

The threshold of the holy of holies in the Egyptian temple may be equated with that of the *huperouranios topos* in Plato's *Phaedrus*, though strictly speaking, the dark inner sanctuary represents the symbolic mound of noetic "creation" in the darkness of Nun. The "prophetic" path leading to liturgic and theurgic unification (later romanticized as a democrat-

80. R.M. van den Berg, *Proclus' Hymns: Essays, Translations, Commentary* (Leiden: Brill, 2001), p. 81.
81. *Ibid.*, p. 63.
82. *Ibid.*, p. 116.

ic and personal *unio mystica*) is closed for ordinary mortals, but open for the living pharaoh and his initiates—both the vindicated and blessed dead (*maa kheru*) and purified living priests, the formal cultic prototypes of the Platonic philosophers and mystics. Lanny Bell states: "The wooden doors of the sanctuary shrine, which enclosed the divine image, were called the 'doors of heaven'. At their opening, ritual participants were projected into the realm of the divine."[83] Here, in the temple's "interior" (*khenu*), all the energy of the divine *bau* that animates the hieratic statues, reliefs and the entire temple is concentrated.

Some nineteenth century scholars may be wrong in imagining the prophet (first of all, the Jewish political moralist and inspired demagogue) as "an exceptional individual and a religious genius",[84] that is, an extraordinary personality who has miraculous inner experiences. In most cases, however, ancient "prophethood" is more like a job appointment—either by the king, or by the patron deity—for the official temple ritual performance and the royal court service. Be that as it may, the prophet (although *de jure* only a humble servant) had an opportunity (or rather, a job requirement) to visit the divine house and see its amazing beauties, or even encounter and glimpse the face of the god himself.

IX

Just as the ancient Near Eastern conception of "prophecy" and "prophethood" (often presented as an instrumental socio-political construct with distinctive literary genres and soteriological implications) may mean different things in dif-

---

83. Lanny Bell *The New Kingdom "Divine" Temple: The Example of Luxor*, Temples of Ancient Egypt, ed. Byron E. Shafer (London: I.B. Tauris, 2005), p. 134.

84. Fritz Stolz, "Dimensions and Transformations of Purification Ideas," in *Transformations of the Inner Self in Ancient Religions*, ed. Jan Assmann and Guy G. Stroumsa (Leiden: Brill, 1999), p. 215.

ferent contexts, so Orpheus may be "all things to all men", according to the deliberately disorienting assertion made by M.L. West, for whom there is only Orphic literature, not Orphism or the Orphics.[85] Standing as a great academic shaman of an astonishing modern Western inanity as regards the Orphic *bakcheia*, West can speak only about "the fashion for claiming Orpheus as an authority", since "the history of Orphism is the history of that fashion."[86]

Although a figure of myth and the preferred name for metaphysical *auctoritas* in telestic and esoteric matters, Orpheus nonetheless appears as a prophet and mystagogue, presumably the "first" to reveal the meaning of the mysteries and rituals of initiation (*teletai*). Since Orphism is an ascetic and telestic way of life, W.K.C. Guthrie surmises that Orpheus did not have a new and entirely distinct species of religion to offer, but rather an esoteric modification and reinterpretation of traditional mythologies, a reformation of Dionysiac energy in the direction of Apollonian sanity: "Those who found it congenial might take him for their prophet, live the Orphic life and call themselves Orphics."[87]

Famous for his charms and incantations (*pharmaka, epodai*), Orpheus appears in countless legendary stories as the son of the solar Apollo and the muse Calliope or as a devoted worshipper of Apollo. Accordingly, Orpheus makes Helios the same as Apollo and Dionysus, though as a giver of oracles and a prophet he always was "companion of Apollo" (*Apollonos hetairon*).[88] Subsequently, Dionysus sent the Maenads against him and he was torn to pieces like the Egyptian Osiris.

---

85. M.L. West, *The Orphic Poems* (Oxford: Clarendon Press, 1983), p. 2.
86. *Ibid.*, p. 3.
87. W.K.C. Guthrie, *Orpheus and Greek Religion: A Study of the Orphic Movement,* with a new Foreword by Larry J. Alderink, (Princeton: Princeton University Press, 1993), p. 9.
88. *Ibid.*, p. 42.

In this respect, however, it needs to be remembered that the "much-labored contrast" between Dionysian and Apollonian dimensions in ancient Mediterranean culture "belongs to German speculation", as A.H. Armstrong rightly observes, rather than to the actual realm of Hellenic piety.[89]

The philosophical "ecstasy" may be sober and passionless, and the utmost "madness" like a supra-noetic metaphysical silence. In a certain sense, the prophetic and poetic frenzy somewhat resembles the epistemic and hermeneutic illumination mediated by the holy light of myths and symbols. These myths—Orphic, Hesiodic and Homeric—may cause a state of Bacchic ecstasy because of their theurgical quality.[90] Therefore, Proclus prays to the Muses that they should bring him to ecstasy through the noeric myths of the sages (*noerois me sophon bakcheusate muthois*: *Hymns* 3.11). And he turns to Athena, the sober patroness of Platonic philosophy, saying: "Give my soul holy light from your sacred myths and wisdom and lore" (*Hymns* 7.33f).[91]

As the paradigmatic lyre player and liturgical singer, Orpheus was also a *theologos* and *theourgos* of sorts. According to some versions of his death, Orpheus was a victim of a thunderbolt from Zeus, since, in a similar way as Prometheus, he taught men things unknown to them before, expounding the mysteries of the soul's descent and ascent.

The lyre and the decapitated head of the murdered Orpheus were thrown into a river and floated across to the island of Lesbos. The temple of Bakchus (the Orphic Dionysus) was built at the spot where the singing and prophesying head of Orpheus was buried. The miraculous lyre had been dedicated at the temple of Apollo, and the singing head became famous as a giver of oracles and prophecies.[92]

---

89. A.H. Armstrong, *The Ancient and Continuing Pieties of the Greek World*, p. 87.

90. R.M. van den Berg, *Proclus' Hymns*, p. 101.

91. *Ibid.*, p. 100.

92. W.K.C. Guthrie, *Orpheus and Greek Religion*, p. 35.

And so, is Orpheus a "prophet" in the trivial sense of a person (or a symbol) who foretells the future, or in the sense of the theological administrator and authority in covenants and treaties of the Israelite politico-military enterprises? In both cases, prophecy is an integral part of the divination whose fundamental cosmological premises and logic are based on the ancient ideology of Near Eastern royalty. Consequently, prophecy is a form of divination along with dreams and visions, as Nissinen indicates: "In the ancient Near East . . . the primary function of all divination was . . . the conviction of the identity, capacity and legitimacy of the ruler and the justification and limitation of his . . . power, based on the communication between the ruler and the god(s)."[93]

Nissinen argues that any definition of prophecy (not just in the widespread cases of literary manifestos and fictions) is a scholarly construct.[94] And a written prophecy is always a scribed construct. The very notion of the human being able to function as a substitute for the animated and speaking divine statue or as an autonomous mouthpiece of the deity is the outcome of particular socio-historical forms and versions of the covenantal patronship. Nissinen writes:

> According to Liddel and Scott's Greek-English Lexicon, *propheteia* is equivalent to the "gift of interpreting the will of gods" and *propheteuo* to being an "interpreter of the gods", whereas *prophetes* is "one who speaks for a God and interprets his will to man", or, generally, an "interpreter". . . . If the word "prophecy", then, can be agreed to denote primarily the activity of transmitting and interpreting the divine will, it can be used as a general concept of related activities in the ancient

---

93. Martti Nissinen, "What is Prophecy? An Ancient Near Eastern Perspective," in *Inspired Speech: Prophecy in the Ancient Near East: Essays in Honor of Herbert B. Huffmon*, ed. John Kaltner and Louis Stulman (New York: Continuum, 2004), p. 21.
94. *Ibid.*, p. 25.

and the modern worlds, independently of its biblical roots and religious affiliations.[95]

X

According to the Hellenic tradition, Pythagoras published his writings in the name of Orpheus. Moreover, like the Orphic initiate, Pythagoras has descended to Hades and returned, coming back through the Delphic sanctuary. Therefore Kingsley surmises that Orpheus, as the inspired mystagogue, "would seem originally to have had the power to fetch the dead back to life",[96] or rather, to lead the dead (meaning the transformed initiates) "into the day of the noetic life of Atum-Ra", or even to "the primeval time before there was any duality".[97] This is a state where Atum, instead of having two eyes (like the paradigmatic Pythagorean dyad), is one-eyed. But the prevailing religious and moral attitudes of the Greeks presumably suppressed Orpheus' initial success and turned it into failure.

Likewise, the (*elletu*) Ishtar, the prototype of the Orphic Persephone, elevates the soul and reintegrates it into the "Pythagorean" decad of the Assyrian sacred tree. This reintegration is analogous to the *baqa* of the Sufis. Being the image of God (like the macrocosmic fullness of the noetic cosmos, the collective of demiurgic archetypes) and the image of the perfect man (*etlu gitmalu*, the microcosmic fullness of the king-initiate-philosopher as a son of God), it is the noetic constellation of divine attributes. The descent and ascent of Ishtar

---

95. *Ibid.*, pp. 19 & 20.

96. Peter Kingsley, *Ancient Philosophy, Mystery, and Magic: Empedocles and Pythagorean Tradition*, p. 226.

97. H. te Velde, "Relations and Conflicts between Egyptian Gods, particularly in the Divine Ennead of Heliopolis," in *Struggles of Gods: Papers of the Groningen Work Group for the Study of the History of Religions*, ed. H.G. Kippenberg in association with H.J.W. Drijvers and Y. Kuiper (Berlin: Mouton Publishers, 1984), p. 250.

had outlined the way for salvation, depicted in terms of the body-like royal tree and the seven-stepped ziggurat tower.[98] And the "numerical" sacred tree of Ishtar itself can be viewed as a graphic representation of both the divine council (*ilani rabuti*) and "cosmic man" as "the human incarnation of the almighty God, Ashur".[99]

According to the ritualized requirement of archetypal *auctoritas*, the early Pythagoreans used to attribute to the prophet Orpheus their own works on the soul's *soteria* (salvation), focused on the figure and fate of Persephone, analogous to the Babylonian and Assyrian Ishtar. And Plato allegedly paraphrased Orpheus and the Orphic literature throughout, according to Olympiodorus' remark: *pantachou gar ho Platon paroidei ta Orpheos*, "Plato paraphrases Orpheus everywhere" (*In Phaed.* 10.3.13). In this respect, Plato simply reshapes and rationalizes the mythical and religious ideas of esoteric Orphism and its Bacchic mysteries of Dionysus. Therefore, Proclus is not so much exaggerating when he claims that Plato received his knowledge of divine matters from Pythagorean and Orphic writings: *ek te ton Puthagoreion kai ton Orphikon grammaton* (*Plat.Theol.* 1.5; *In Tim.* III.160.17-161.6).[100]

Like Orpheus, Plato's Socrates is a servant of Apollo, maintaining that the best music is philosophy. Hence, philosophical talk is analogous to the prophetic song of Orpheus or the theological hymn of "Apollo's philosophical swan who sings that this life is a prelude to a disincarnate afterlife".[101]

The Orphic myth (or the philosophical Platonic myth) can serve us if we obey it, following the upper road, and if we regard it as a model for present behaviour in accordance

---

98. Simo Parpola, *Assyrian Prophecies*, p. XCV.

99. Simo Parpola, "Monotheism in Ancient Assyria," in *One God or Many? Concepts of Divinity in the Ancient World*, ed. Barbara Nevling Porter (Chebeague, ME: Transactions of the Casco Bay Assyriological Institute, 2000), p. 190.

100. Peter Kingsley, *ibid.*, p. 131.

101. Kathryn A. Morgan, *Myth and Philosophy from the Presocratics to Plato* (Cambridge: Cambridge University Press, 2000), p. 196.

with the revealed knowledge of the afterlife. This knowledge is about the soul's judgement and the very depths of Duat, the Osirian netherworld, where Ra and Osiris unite at the deepest point in the nocturnal journey of the Egyptian solar barque. Thoth is seated in front of the barque, attending to the Eye of Horus and healing it. And the solar barque itself is transformed into a holy serpent "whose fiery breath pierces a pathway through the otherwise impenetrable gloom".[102] As Kathryn Morgan relates: "The myth teaches us that we must try to retain as much memory of the world beyond as possible."[103]

Accordingly, Pythagoras worships Apollo-Helios (the Sun as an icon of the divine Intellect) because of knowledge acquired in the dark Osirian underworld. Pythagoras emerged from Persephone's realm as an immortalized hierophant of Orpheus, the revealer of the Pythagorean "holy sacraments". In sum, he is like Dionysus restored and Osiris united with Ra in the netherworld, because the true philosopher (and the Egyptian royal initiate) is the "deceased" who "sees the god and knows his secret".[104] He is "dead" to the illusory world of impermanence, corruption and ignorance. Hence, the Orphico-Platonic philosopher contemplates the eternal Ideas and is himself mingled with the gods. As Erik Hornung observes:

Having become a god, the deceased resides where the gods reside and may encounter them face to face. While still on earth the gods are approached only indirectly, through images and symbols. One such symbol is the sun, but only in

102. Erik Hornung, *The Ancient Egyptian Books of the Afterlife*, tr. David Lorton (Ithaca and London: Cornell University Press, 1999), pp. 36-37.

103. Kathryn A. Morgan, *ibid.*, p. 209.

104. Erik Hornung, *Idea into Image: Essays on Ancient Egyptian Thought*, tr. Elizabeth Bredeck (New York: Timken Publishers, 1992), p. 112.

the depths of the underworld can humans actually meet the sun in person.[105]

XI

In certain traditional accounts, Orpheus is depicted as the grandson of the king Charops, to whom Dionysus—when invading Europe from Asia—has given the kingdom and has taught the mystic rites of initiation related to the later mysteries of Eleusis. Orpheus himself almost merged with the lyre-playing god Apollo, and consequently he was able to charm all nature and tame the wildest of beasts with his playing and singing—his "sacred incantations" (*hieron epaoidon*) and prayers (*euchai*). Birds and animals came to hear Orpheus' music, and even trees were calmed.

One should remember that dancing and flute or lyre music were traditional parts of the sacrificial cult of Apollo, and these Apollonian musical rituals held a privileged place in ancient Hellenic religion. According to Johannes Quasten:

> Orpheus was considered by the ancient world to be the representative of cultic music. . . . Music had the same character of epiclesis. It was supposed to "call down" the good gods . . . because song and music increased the efficacy of the epiclesis the words of epiclesis were nearly always sung to instrumental accompaniment. Thus the Dionysian fellowship used the so-called *humnoi kletikoi* of women in order to obtain the appearance of their god.[106]

The practice of Pythagorean and Platonic philosophy is itself tantamount to the singing of rationally composed ana-

---

105. *Ibid.*, p. 110.

106. Johannes Quasten, *Music and Worship in Pagan and Christian Antiquity*, tr. Boniface Ramsey (Washington, D.C: National Association of Pastoral Musicians, 1983), pp. 10 & 17.

gogic hymns, thus imitating Apollo, the Leader of the Muses. The Muses sometimes are equated with the *anagogion phos*, the elevating light that kindles the soul with *anagogion pur*, the upward-leading fire. For Proclus, the prayer-like hymns are "theurgical instruments",[107] and "human philosophy is an imitation of Apollo's hymns."[108]

Orpheus, as the paradigmatic itinerant seer, is credited for the ability to pacify through his music, to heal, to foretell the future and interpret the past, as well as shape the traditions of the gods—theology in the form of myths, spells and epic songs. Arguing that both Thales' and Orpheus' music worked magic, Neta Ronen attributes special healing powers to the song of Orpheus as it is described by Apollonius Rhodius. Presumably, the theogony which he performed itself had the power to restore cosmic and social harmony.[109]

Plato's dialogues themselves may be viewed as a product of "musical madness", constructed following the rules of dialectical reasoning and logic. Hence, philosophy, as an artful strategy of recollection and restoration of vision, "is related to the performance arts of dancing and love poetry".[110]

Both philosophical dialectic and esoterically interpreted myth produce the *logos* which is an image of the higher noetic and henadic reality. This reality itself is beyond the adequate capture either by *muthos* or by *logos*, each of which are by degrees representations—plausible (*eikos*) perhaps, but ultimately open to the risk of deception or misinterpretation. Likewise, and with a similar imaginative splendour, the ineffable essence of wisdom (if not of being) may be revealed by the cosmic choreography and theurgic music of the calendrical festivals and seasons. This kind of telestic dance-theatre

---

107. R.M. van den Berg, *Proclus' Hymns*, p. 33.

108. *Ibid.*, p. 23.

109. Neta Ronen, "Who Practiced Purification in Archaic Greece? A Cultural Profile," in *Transformations of the Inner Self in Ancient Religions*, ed. Jan Assmann and Guy G. Stroumsa (Leiden: Brill, 1999), p. 284.

110. Kathryn A. Morgan, *Myth and Philosophy from the Presocratics to Plato*, p. 235.

is established for the sake of the circular descent and ascent, manifestation and the return to the source. According to Gregory Shaw:

> Musical theurgy was a form of anamnesis that awakened the soul to its celestial identity with the gods. . . . Musical theurgy came from the gods and gave the soul direct contact with them. . . . According to Iamblichus, Pythagoras was the first composer of this anagogic music. . . . The sacred names and incantations used in theurgic invocations also originated from the gods, and Iamblichus says the Egyptian prophet Bitys revealed "the name of the god that pervades the entire cosmos" (*De myster.* 268.2-3). . . . For Iamblichus the god whose "name" pervaded the cosmos was Helios. . . . Man's prayers must therefore be presented to Helios through the many zodiacal schemata that the god assumes. Iamblichus says: "The Egyptians employ these sorts of prayers to Helios not only in their visions but also in their more ordinary prayers that have this same kind of meaning, and they are offered to God according to this symbolic mystagogy" (*De myster.* 254.6-10).[111]

In the later Pythagorean milieu, the seven strings of Orpheus' lyre are connected with the seven circles of heaven, suggesting that "the souls need the cithara in order to ascend."[112] The theory of the seven vowels and the seven-string cosmic lyre, related to the different planets, colours, sounds and the seasonal rotation of the year, is perhaps of Babylonian origin. It is also related to Egypt as the ultimate source of the main (or least initial) esoteric principles of esoteric Orphic lore.

The use of lyre or cithara music during the rites of ascension is attested along with the mantric intoning of the seven vowels that allegedly enabled the soul to escape the darkness of the irrational lower existence and return to the divine

---

111. Gregory Shaw, *Theurgy and the Soul: The Neoplatonism of Iamblichus* (University Park: Pennsylvania State University Press, 1995), pp. 175-77.
112. M.L. West, *The Orphic Poems*, p. 30.

realm from which it initially descended. The theurgic way of
the Orphic *bakcheia* (initiation, recollection, reintegration, elevation to the solar noetic realm) is provided for the Orphic
and Bacchic initiates (*orphikoi, bakchoi*), those who looked to
Orpheus as their prophet and practised *bios Orphikos* or *bios
Puthagorikos*.

The Egyptian provenance of this purificatory way of life
(*bios*)—and here it is only the archetypal ideal, not the actual
transmission that matters—is affirmed by Herodotus when he
speaks about the Egyptian custom of wearing linen tunics:
"They agree in this with the observances which are called Orphic and Bacchic, but are in fact Egyptian and Pythagorean"
(*Hist.* 2.81).[113]

Burkert also recognized that although Orpheus wove together and melded different Near Eastern traditions (Akkadian, Hurrite-Hittite), the Egyptian metaphysical and cultic tradition is used most of all.[114] It is evident that not only
Egyptian cosmogonies, but also the royal paths of salvation—
popularized through the temple initiations, hermeneutical instructions and educational programmes related to the Egyptian Book of the Dead—are reshaped and reused, though for
the Greek audience the Egyptian illustrations "seem to be
even more suggestive than the Egyptian formulas".[115]

XII

The so-called Orphic and Pythagorean spiritual revolution
consists in a reversion of the traditional Greek view, namely, that *psuche* is a simulacrum (*eidolon*) of the mortal body.
The Orphic and pro-Egyptian Dionysical-Osirian esoterism
now regards the living body as an illusory and transitory (al-

113. *Ibid.*, p. 16.
114. Walter Burkert, *Babylon, Memphis, Persepolis: Eastern Contexts of Greek Culture* (Cambridge, MA: Harvard University Press, 2004), p. 98.
115. *Ibid.*, p. 87.

beit complex and complicated) image of the immortal soul, whose purification may be described as separation from the body (*soma*, corpse) by recollection (*anamnesis*), asceticism (turning away from the flux of becoming, *ta genomena*, and from its unreliable images), and philosophical contemplation (*theoria*) of intelligible principles.

In short, the prospect of personal immortality in the Egyptian fashion and promotion of "scientific knowledge" (*episteme*) as the chief soteriological power are inseparable from their initial Orphico-Pythagorean context. Though "the idea of proof is introduced as a rhetorical device,"[116] not related with *theoria* as a spectacle of the divine epiphany, science and logic can claim to constitute the salvation of its practitioners only when based on the premise of the mathematical nature of the demiurgic world-construction.

The "scientific" soteriology of Plato, itself based on the Pythagorean and Sophistic *episteme*, is a domain of a small elite group whose critical reflections and ironic speculations in relation to the central body of political orthodoxy and the Sophistic style of education are regarded as an almost gnosis-like means of "dialectical salvation". Yehuda Elkana explains:

> For instance, the road to the Pythagorean heaven leads through the well-defined corpus of the geometrical proof. This is the Pythagorean soteriology. . . . The carriers of the transcendental vision are small groups of intellectuals, often marginal to society, who contemplate the alternative views of the world. . . . The moment when the logos—which is not bestowed upon every person in the same degree . . . —is becoming the main source of knowledge, then the source of knowledge becomes elitist and authoritarian by nature. Consequently, it is not surprising that the fields that were built upon the Parmenidean method, that is, by strict deductions—

---

116. Yehuda Elkana, "The Emergence of Second Order Thinking in Classical Greece," in *The Origins and Diversity of Axial Age Civilizations*, ed. S.N. Eisenstadt (Albany: State University of New York Press, 1986), p. 61.

namely mathematics and theoretical physics—became strictly authoritarian, and their practitioners began to organize themselves into exclusive groups like the Academy, the Lyceum, and some monastic orders: all these are characterized by equality among the members and authoritarian separatism towards the outside world.[117]

Since the Homeric values of body-life and shadow- or simulacrum-like soul are radically inverted by their esoteric opponents, what survives now is the soul understood as a manifestation (*ba* in the Egyptian Ramesside theology)[118] of the divine spirit—be it called *daimon* or *theos*. The soul as the winged *ba* (the breath and living image of Amun) alone is from the gods. Therefore, "what survives is an image of life (*eidolon aionos*), which sleeps during normal bodily consciousness but wakes up while the body sleeps and foresees future events in prophetic dreams."[119]

The soul as a sort of fallen *daimon*, or as a Dionysian divine spark, is buried in a tomb-like material body, thus entering the cosmic cycle of elemental transformation. Hence, the soul is the pre-existing and immortal knowing subject. It passes through a number of incarnations in a cyclical pattern, and these bodily incarnations may be regarded as a sort of punishment, ordeal, or simply viewed as a result of forgetfulness, ignorance and play.

Therefore, the ultimate aim of the soul is freedom from the wheel of terrestrial punishment following the soteriological formula *bios-thanatos-bios* (life-death-life), which shows the way of entering the eternal and noetic "day" of Ra or Helios. This freedom implies the restoration of one's initial divine

117. *Ibid.*, pp. 43, 47 & 55.

118. Jan Assmann, *Moses the Egyptian: The Memory of Egypt in Western Monotheism* (Cambridge, MA: Harvard University Press, 2002), pp. 197-206.

119. K. Corrigan, "Body and Soul in Ancient Religious Experience," in *Classical Mediterranean Spirituality: Egyptian, Greek, Roman*, ed. A.H. Armstrong (London: Routledge and Kegan Paul, 1986), p. 364.

identity. The deliverance (*lusis*) is performed by Dionysus Bakchios through specific cathartic rituals; and Persephone must decide whether those purified souls that have paid the penalty for their wrongful deeds may be sent to the "seats of the blessed" (*hedras eis euhageon*).[120] The soul's ultimate goal is its final liberation from the painful cycle of reincarnation, thus arriving "at the victor's crown with swift feet" and ending as god instead of mortal.[121]

As Bartel Poortman observes, it is the Orphico-Pythagorean tradition that Socrates has in mind when he introduces the theory of recollection (*anamnesis*), experienced by certain divinely inspired seers and poets, and based on the clear separation of the immortal soul and mortal body:

> This ontological dualism goes hand in hand with epistemological dualism. There are two different states of knowing: having the Forms for its objects, *psuche*'s state is *episteme*; having the *aistheta* for its objects, the senses' state of knowing is *doxa*. The fact of having the Forms as objects of knowledge implies that *psuche* is immortal. This is in line with the principle known from the Presocratic "theory of knowledge" *similia similibus* (*cognoscuntur*): the Forms are imperishable, therefore the subject knowing them must be imperishable.[122]

This subject contemplates the Forms like the temple *prophetes* contemplates the animated hieratic statues of the Egyptian gods. His own eye (*iret*) is awakened to light and related to the active aspect (*iru*, "that which acts") of the visible

---

120. Fritz Graf, "Dionysian and Orphic Eschatology: New Texts and Old Questions," in *Masks of Dionysus*, ed. Thomas H. Carpenter and Christopher A. Faraone (Ithaca and London: Cornell University Press, 1993), p. 253.

121. *Ibid.*, p. 254.

122. Bartel Poortman, "Death and Immortality in Greek Philosophy: From the Presocratics to the Hellenistic Era," in *Hidden Futures: Death and Immortality in Ancient Egypt, Anatolia, the Classical, Biblical and Arabic-Islamic World*, ed. J.M. Bremer, Theo. P.J. van den Hout and Rudolph Peters (Amsterdam: Amsterdam University Press, 1994), pp. 209-10.

manifestation of the deity through the shining light. So the ability of the cult statue (the *tut* of Amun, for example) to act (*iri*) is a response to the ritual action, equated with the Eye of Horus and performed by the priest. The cobra-like *uraeus* of the animated statue is identified with the solar Eye of the divine self-consciousness and with *maat* (truth, right proportion and justice). Even the officiant "refers to himself as a *ba* and as the goddess Sekhmet" at the point when he is ready to embrace the statue.[123]

The Platonic subject imagines the vision of these Forms by himself when he is unrestricted by a mortal body, that is, either after physical death, or whilst living in the body and "separation" is accomplished by the Osirian initiation or by a kind of philosophical contemplation (*theoria*). This telestic or dialectical "separation" is regarded as essentially an intellective (*noeric*) passage. It is like one's entering the solar barque of Ra, based on the ontological and epistemological premise that embodied cognition mirrors disembodied cognition, or rather divine intellection. Consequently, only when separated from our mortal bodies and elevated to the stars (the henadic archetypes) do we regain our true divine identity, our real being and "gnostic immortality", being in an ideal cognitional (or rather contemplative) state of knowledge (*episteme*).

Since the ideal Platonic knower is the disembodied soul, analogous to the Egyptian *ba* turned into the noetic *akh*, Plato's Socrates elaborates an eschatological Orphic myth of the blessed afterlife after separation of body and soul and "the identification of the person with the latter", for "it is the state of the latter that is judged by the gods."[124] Therefore, Lloyd Gerson argues: "For Plato, embodied persons are the only

---

123. David Lorton, "The Theology of Cult Statues in Ancient Egypt," in *Born in Heaven, Made on Earth: The Making of the Cult Image in the Ancient Near East*, ed. Michael B. Dick (Winona Lake, IN: Eisenbrauns, 1999), p. 141.

124. Lloyd P. Gerson, *Knowing Persons: A Study in Plato* (Oxford: Oxford University Press, 2003), p. 26.

sorts of images that can reflexively recognize their own relatively inferior states as images and strive to transform themselves into their own ideal."[125]

Hence, philosophers "long to die" and strive to transform themselves into the *akhu*—the noetic spirits of light that participate in the Sun god's resurrection and share "the triumph of Ra".[126] They stipulate this metaphorical and literal "separation" by means of a certain epistemological initiation, since the philosopher's soul "attains truth" by "reasoning" (*to logizesthai: Phaed.* 65b.9).

XIII

The impure cannot conjoin with the pure, since the latter is without impurity. Accordingly, either wisdom (*phronesis*) and knowledge (*episteme*) are nowhere to be gained, or else it is for the dead, for the Egyptian *maa kheru* who sees the god (Osiris-Ra) and knows his secret by undergoing a symbolic death: "He becomes an initiate, as in the later mystery cults that derive many of their notions from ancient Egyptian concepts of death and the hereafter."[127]

In addition, all his members (like the parts of the restored Eye of Horus) are equated with divinities and thereby constructed as an ideal icon, as an ideal statue-like image of Osiris, thus becoming entirely a god. According to Hornung, although the term *akh* is written with the hieroglyph of a crested ibis (*ibis comata*, the sign of Thoth, whose telestic wisdom includes the ability to use the transformative *heka* power, *heka*

---

125. *Ibid.*, p. 4.

126. Henk Milde, "'Going out into the Day': Ancient Egyptian Beliefs and Practices concerning Death," in *Hidden Futures: Death and Immortality in Ancient Egypt, Anatolia, the Classical, Biblical and Arabic-Islamic World*, ed. J.M. Bremer, Theo. P.J. van den Hout and Rudolph Peters (Amsterdam: Amsterdam University Press, 1994), p. 34.

127. Erik Hornung, *Idea into Image: Essays on Ancient Egyptian Thought*, p. 112.

being the *ba* of Ra), the *akh* is usually depicted not as a bird, but as a mummy, the ideal *sah*-body, tantamount to one's archetypal *eidos* made visible. Hornung states:

> A person can become an *akh* only after death, and descriptions of the afterlife differentiate clearly between *akh*s, the blessed dead and those dead persons who have been judged and condemned. Related to the Egyptian verb meaning "to illuminate", the term *akh* is usually translated as "transfigured one", for it is through a process of ritual transfigurations that the deceased becomes an *akh*.[128]

In this way the knower becomes what he knows, and is transformed into the noetic light whose idealized bodily image (the statue-sanctuary) adequately reflects a particular divine Form. The body of the transformed initiate, even before his physical passing away, is tantamount to the Osirian *sah*-body (mummy), to the *sunthema*-like tomb, and able to serve as a receptacle for the divine *ba*. Understood in this sense, the tomb is analogous to the womb-like primaeval mound of Heliopolis, and the philosopher inside this alchemical tomb (like Phanes inside the cosmic egg) is the vehicle of transformation, of one's own turning into the god-like *akh*. Eventually, it means becoming not what one is not, but rather restoring one's real noetic identity by moving from image to reality, from the sensible things that are "unlike" (*anomoion*) to their paradigmatic spiritual "likeness". Therefore, Gerson writes:

> Paradoxically, renunciation of worldly concerns—the practice and the goal of philosophy—is literally metaphorical dying. It will turn out that what differentiates embodied persons from other images is that they are able to be self-conscious of their status as images. As one "dies to the body", one comes to recognize oneself as a living metaphor for what is really real. The

---

128. *Ibid.*, p. 184.

recognition is identical to the construction of an ideal self in so far as that is possible for the embodied person.[129]

According to Plato, only the rational part of the soul (*logistikon*) sees the Ideas, and as a result, only this part of the soul is immortal. In the *Phaedrus* myth it is represented by the charioteer able to contemplate and be nourished by the Parmenidean noetic world which alone "really and truly is".

Plato's theory of the soul's immortality, of its reincarnation through the cosmic cycle of becoming and its ultimate salvation by the means of recollection and dialectical ascent, is an inseparable part of his erotic *philosophia*. The "lover of wisdom" tries to imitate (*mimeisthai*) the Forms, thus making himself a likeness of them, "realizing one's nature by actually identifying with the immaterial".[130] By becoming like the noetic *eidos*, he becomes one out of the many. For Plato, this process consequently:

> . . . generally takes 10,000 years before *psuche* has regrown its wings and may return to its heavenly home. The philosopher, however, is in an exceptional position: in his case it takes 3,000 years. After every thousand years there is to be a new reincarnation, partly determined by lot, partly by choice. The period between a life and a new incarnation is the time to be punished or rewarded. The first incarnation will be in a human body; subsequent incarnations may be in animal bodies. The philosopher's cycle is completed sooner because his life is dominated by a constant devotion to the Forms; . . . only the philosopher's *psuche* regrows its wings.[131]

This Platonic "science" of transmigration (*metoikesis*) and metempsychosis is typically out of favour with modern schol-

---

129. Lloyd P. Gerson, *Knowing Persons: A Study in Plato*, pp. 57-58.
130. *Ibid.*, p. 129.
131. Bartel Poortman, *Death and Immortality in Greek Philosophy: From the Presocratics to the Hellenistic Era*, p. 213.

ars and discounted as an exotic curiosity. Its presumably Egyptian links are uncertain. Hornung argues with considerable persuasion that the writers of antiquity, when presented with the so-called *ba*-theology and its role in all kinds of miraculous transformations, "mistakenly thought that the Egyptians believed in metempsychosis or the transmigration of the soul".[132]

However, in its Platonic form this theory is based on the entirely new soteriological perspective that amalgamated the ancient Egyptian royal concept of noetic (astral and solar) immortality with Neo-Assyrian and Neo-Babylonian astronomy, and perhaps the Indian Shramanic (Jainic, Upanishadic) path of perfection. Neither the traditional Greek religion nor Homer teach the tripartite cosmological doctrine of reincarnation, wandering "far from the blessed company of gods", and release. The theories of reincarnation appeared in Greece around the seventh or sixth centuries BC as the Orphic myth of the soul as an exiled god wandering through the four elements—or through all the forms of nature (*pantoia eidea thneton*, according to Empedocles, fr. 115.7). This soul seeks to return to the company of the gods through asceticism, telestic sacraments and philosophy, in the hope of an early release from the wheel of birth and death. As Thomas McEvilley observes, regarding the Orphico-Pythagorean milieu of Ameinias the Pythagorean and his disciple Parmenides:

> The Goddess Dike Polypoinos, "Justice with Many Punishments," adopted by Parmenides, is otherwise known only as an Orphic goddess (who may have had to do with enforcing karmic consequences in the arrangement of rebirths). If Parmenides held a variant of the tripartite doctrine of reincarnation, then the "peace" for which he thanked Ameinias could only be release from reincarnation—the state of *jivan-mukta*.[133]

---

132. Erik Hornung, *Idea into Image*, p. 183.
133. Thomas McEvilley, *The Shape of Ancient Thought: Comparative Studies in Greek and Indian Philosophies* (New York: Allworth Press, 2002), p. 111.

The mystic opportunity to reach the interior divine presence—directly and immediately—is tantamount to the miraculous leap beyond the macrocosmic circle of *ouranos*. This is an exceptional release before the ending of the cosmic cycle and in spite of the rules of necessity. According to Peter Manchester:

> The question shifted from that of one's status among the dead, in an afterlife that was real in the same way as successive cycles of Eternal Return, to that of whether one had awakened, in *this* life, to a transcending spiritual and interior life that knows its own eternity already and in death is released from the cycle of birth and death and from worldly existence altogether.[134]

The Orphic cult (*telete*), with all its prominent purifications and initiations, was far more private and esoteric than the Hellenic public festivals and mysteries, politically and spiritually centred around the Delphic sanctuary. The new model of post-Homeric political culture sharply distinguished public life from private life, viewing public life as superior, more rational and more important.[135] Since the cosmos, and likewise ordered human society, were both rationalized in various ways, the inner religious life (suddenly discovered as a path of release) became associated with the private sphere and marginal esoteric movements. Orpheus and Pythagoras in varying degrees responded to the demand for logical thought. Both these mystagogues became much more sym-

---

134. Peter Manchester, "The Religious Experience of Time and Eternity," in *Classical Mediterranean Spirituality: Egyptian, Greek, Roman*, ed. A.H. Armstrong (London: Routledge & Kegan Paul, 1986), p. 392.

135. S.C. Humpreys, "Dynamics of the Greek Breakthrouugh: The Dialogue Between Philosophy and Religion," in *The Origins and Diversity of Axial Age Civilizations*, ed. S.N. Eisenstadt (Albany: State University of New York Press, 1986), p. 95.

bols of *auctoritas* than persons of reliable historical biography:

> But both offered a new kind of knowledge about the after-
> life and new theories about the nature of the universe, which
> had a more "scientific" tone than the traditional cosmologies.
> Both emphasized in their teaching, and in the dietary rules
> which accompanied it, the separation between the believers
> and the rest of the world, the uninitiated. Both rejected ani-
> mal sacrifice, the major rite of traditional religion.[136]

Hence, the deeper religious life comes to be associated with the private and non-political realm, beyond the socially demanding framework of the *polis*. Both telestic activities and theological beliefs became a matter of personal choice, and an interiorized "spiritual" existence started to be wholly devoted to religious purification or particular philosophical practises. Likewise, an innovative Parmenidean and Platonic philosophy was practiced and developed by a tiny esoteric minority of Apollo's devotees, dissidents and reformers. In this case, both the way of ritual elevation and that of dialectical ascent were aspiring to the same *telos*: to a transcendent and immanent presence of the divine self-identity. In addition, according to K. Corrigan, Plato inherited and reused:

> 1) the Pythagorean theory that there is an eternal order un-
> derlying sensible reality which is expressible in number, har-
> mony, and geometrical pattern; and 2) the Orphic-Pythagore-
> an idea that the soul is a fallen god, imprisoned in the body,
> which existed before birth and which can after death realize
> its divinity.[137]

---

136. *Ibid.*, p. 9.
137. K. Corrigan, *Body and Soul in Ancient Religious Experience*, p. 374.

XIV

Those initiates (*mustai*) who called themselves *bakchoi* looked to Orpheus as their prophet, depicting him as sent by the deity as a revealer of truth about the soul, life after death, and salvation. Hence, Orpheus was viewed as the founder of the soteriological rites (*teletai*) of Dionysus Bakchois (who sends his telestic *mania* and unhinges the supplicants into madness) and Dionysus Lusios (who frees from madness and transmigration). These *lusioi teletai* of Bakchios are centred on purification as an art of "separation".[138]

West assumes that the Bacchic and Pythagorean Orphica probably represent two parallel developments from a common field of origin. At the same time he presupposes a conceptual link between Pherecydes of Syros (the famous seer who promulgated the theory of metempsychosis and, allegedly, brought together the poems of Orpheus) and Pythagoras.[139]

The Orphic doctrines are fragmentarily attested by the golden leaves and plates that bear testimony of the Orphic preparation for death, analogous to the *paideia* provided by the Egyptian officiants of the House of Life (*per ankh*), those who composed, recited and ritually performed the Book of the Dead (*pert em hru*). In Egypt, death is regarded as a way to real life in the realm of *akhu*.

Like the nocturnal Ra, the deceased "philosopher-king" is transformed into a scarab and a child encircled by the ouroboric serpent "who burns millions". The Egyptian-Hermetic illumination-regeneration "appears as the mystery which saves", and its central motif consists in the noetic vision, "fol-

---

138. Walter Burkert, "Bacchic Teletai in the Hellenistic Age," in *Masks of Dionysus*, ed. Thomas H. Carpenter and Christopher A. Pharaone (Ithaca and London: Cornell University Press, 1993), p. 273.

139. M. L. West, *The Orphic Poems*, pp. 18-20.

lowing an ancient model of cosmic journey which is, actually, an interior journey".[140]

According to the Egyptians, both humans and gods originate in the all-embracing deity, the One Alone, though the gods issue from Atum's sweat and humans from his tears. As Assmann observes, these primaeval "humans" are probably referred to in a way that means "clients", that is, those who at the beginning appear as the community of the noetic flock, the primordial "saints" (the Sufi *awliya*). In this sense, they are "contemplators", "knowers", "philosophers" here below as Atum-Ra is above, after heaven is raised up on high (at the end of a golden age) and the gods are separated from fallen humanity.[141]

As the embodied beings whose *telos* is to restore the perfect state of solar contemplation, humans are "oracular creatures"[142] for whose sake the world was created as the theurgic theatre of the divine Eye. The creation is accomplished (or rather constantly "performed") by the thinking heart (intellect), and then by the speaking tongue (logos) and by writing or drawing (*ta hieragrammata*, the writing of divine speech: *sesh en medu neter*). According to Assmann:

> Writing only carries out what is already implicit in the structure of reality. This structure is "hieroglyphic". It is a kind of Platonism. Plato interprets the visible world as the infinite material impression of a finite set of immaterial ideas. The Egyptians interpreted the visible world as a kind of infinitely ongoing series production which very faithfully follows an

140. Giovanni Filoramo, *The Transfiguration of the Inner Self in Gnostic and Hermetic Texts: Transformations of the Inner Self in Ancient Religions*, ed. Jan Assmann and Guy G. Stroumsa (Leiden: Brill, 1999), pp. 143 & 145.
141. Jan Assmann, *Egyptian Solar Religion in the New Kingdom: Re, Amun and the Crisis of Polytheism* (London and New York: Kegan Paul International, 1995), p. 165.
142. *Ibid.*, p. 169.

original finite set of types or models. And this same set is also represented by the hieroglyphic system.[143]

To be restored as the hieroglyph of the Eye means to enter the solar barque of Ra and join his all-embracing noetic contemplation by means of the life-giving rays. The Orphic text on the golden tablet from the grave of Thessalian Petroporos conveys the similar claim: "Now you have died and now you have come into being, O thrice happy one, on this same day. Tell Persephone that Bakchios himself has set you free."[144]

The blessed deceased emerges into the realm of divine being when his mortal body passes away. He is invited to the holy symposium of the gods in order to enjoy "eternal drunkenness", according to a mocking remark made by Plato (*Rep.* 363cd).[145] This "drunkenness" in the company of the re-divinised "Orphic saints" is, in fact, tantamount to the noetic bliss of the Osirian *olbioi* (the "blessed ones"), those who received "a gift of Memory" (*Mnemosunes doron*). The blessed ones appear in the form of *akh* in the court of Ra, where Setne's *ba* is going in hope "to see the future" and "get information from the gods".[146]

The Egyptian goddess Hathor initiates the ascent to heaven and is depicted as "rising in turquoise from the eastern horizon" (CT 486).[147] Hathor (the "House of Horus") is the goddess of ecstatic drunkenness, dance and music. But her essential hypostasis is the fiery Eye of Ra. She is the *Iret*-Eye that "acts as the agent of the god's activity".[148] The deceased

143. *Ibid.*, p. 174.

144. Fritz Graf, *Dionysian and Orphic Eschatology: New Texts and Old Questions*, p. 241.

145. *Ibid.*, p. 246.

146. John Gee, "Oracle by Image: Coffin Text 103 in Context," in *Magic and Divination in the Ancient World*, ed. Leda Ciraolo and Jonathan Seidel (Leiden: Brill/Styx, 2002), p. 84.

147. Alison Roberts, *Hathor Rising: The Serpent Power of Ancient Egypt* (Rottingdean: Northgate Publishers, 2001), p. 10.

148. *Ibid.*, p. 9.

or the initiate—the "one who knows things" (*rekh (a)khet*), the sage (*remet-rekh*)—is equated not only with Osiris, but also with Hathor, thus immortalised as the "solar gaze" and the fiery beauty (*nefer*) of truth (*maat*).

XV

In Greece, Orpheus, Linus, Musaeus and other "revealers of mysteries" proclaim the programme of salvation, presenting Persephone-Kore and Dionysus, for instance, as saviours of mankind. This "Greece" of Orpheus is not the scholarly construct that depicts the eulogised tiny city-state of Athens— incomparable with either the highly bureaucratised state of Late Period Egypt[149] or with the Neo-Assyrian cosmopolis and its Persian imitations. Rather, Orpheus belonged to the world of wandering *demiourgoi*—the performers of purifications (*katharmoi*) and initiations (*teletai*), the seers, singers and healers able to discover the "ancient guilt" (*palaion menima*). As Burkert relates:

> Orphic anthropogony . . . has the story of the most ancient and most general kind of *menima* inherent in man as such, the "ancient grief of Persephone" in the words of Pindar. . . . The myth, especially when combined with the doctrine of transmigration and the ensuing ascetic life-style, could have been the basis for a religion of salvation.[150]

The seers and magicians claimed to be able to restore the imagined ideal state of *harmonia*, governed by the "universal

---

149. Tom Hare, *Remembering Osiris: Number, Gender, and the Word in Ancient Egyptian Representational Systems* (Stanford, CA: Stanford University Press, 1999), p. 289.

150. Walter Burkert, "Craft Versus Sect: The Problem of Orphics and Pythagoreans," in *Jewish and Christian Self-Definition, Vol.3: Self-Definition in the Graeco-Roman World*, ed. Ben F. Meyer and E.P. Sanders (London: SCM Press, 1982), pp. 8-9.

law", the Vedic *rta*, as "the unifying principle which animates the parts into a single cosmic machine",[151] like the animated "chariot of truth" (*harma dikes*; Sanskrit *ratham rtasya*) drawn by a pair of horses—the divine twins.

Similarly, Parmenides speaks about the axle of the chariot on which he rides. He mentions the "rounded wheels" (*kukloi*), or the "whirling wheels" that can bring him to the great open threshold where the *Heliades kourai*, daughters of the Sun, hasten to the light revealed through the Eye's rounded pupil. Hence, the symbol of *helios* (of the Egyptian *aten*, viewed as egg of the primaeval fire) is the rounded sound-like image of *kosmos noetos*, the object of contemplation and theurgic glorification for the Thothian apes of the Sun, the Eastern *bau*: "Their importance lies in the fact that they represent the divine community of worshippers of the sun god, whose ranks the sun priest joins with his hymn. By praying to the sun he becomes one of them."[152]

Orpheus, as the archetypal singer, prophet, priest and healer, reconciles the one and the many with his "prophetic lyre" and through the song of harmony (*tes harmonias te ode*). The later Byzantine tradition describes the divine Logos as producing a kind of miraculous music which, by means of "the *iunx* of resonance" (*iunx* meaning both the *iunx*-bird and the magic *iunx*-wheel),[153] has the ability to charm (*katakelon*) and attract (*methelkomenos*) the human soul.[154] These *iunges* (plural of *iunx*), sometimes referred to as "tongues of the gods",

151. John Curtis Franklin, "Harmony in Greek and Indo-Iranian Cosmology," in *The Journal of Indo-European Studies*, vol. 30, nos 1 & 2, Spring/Summer 2002, p. 8.

152. Jan Assmann, *Egyptian Solar Religion in the New Kingdom*, p. 24.

153. See Algis Uždavinys, *Philosophy and Theurgy in Late Antiquity* (San Rafael, CA: Sophia Perennis, 2010), pp. 107-18; Sarah Iles Johnston, *Hekate Soteira: A Study of Hekate's Roles in the Chaldean Oracles and Related Literature* (Atlanta: Scholars Press, 1990), pp. 90-110 (ch. VII: "Hekate's Top and the Iynx-Wheel").

154. Sarah Iles Johnston, "The Song of the Iynx: Magic and Rhetoric in Pythian 4," in *Transactions of the American Philological Association 125*, 1995, p. 183.

are the four-spoked wheels of brass, iron or gold, hanging from the ceilings of temples and capable of producing a seductive sound like that of the Sirens. As a result, they functioned as instruments of the divine voice, an important aspect in theurgy (viewed by Sarah Johnston as "a form of Platonic mysticism"): "The sounds produced by *iynges* whirled by the theurgists were understood to affect and influence not only individuals and objects on earth, but the heavenly bodies as well."[155]

Likewise, Orpheus' music and voice may stir human beings, animals, trees, stones, and even the gods—Persephone herself is charmed, and therefore allows him to bring up his dead wife from Hades. The enchanting Orphic song is somewhat analogous to the wind sound produced by an *iunx*-wheel: its *peitho dolia*—the charmed power of persuasion and seduction that tricks[156]—belongs to Orpheus' divine instrument, his lyre. Nicomachus of Gerasa, the Neopythagorean scholar, describes it as follows:

> Hermes invented the lyre from the tortoise-shell, and providing it with seven strings, handed down the art of lyre-playing to Orpheus. And Orpheus taught Thamyris and Linus. Linus taught Heracles, by whom he was killed. He also taught Amphion, the Theban, who built Thebes with seven gates after the seven strings of the lyre. When Orpheus was killed by the Thracian women, his lyre was thrown into the sea and was cast up in the city of Antissa in Lesbos. Fishermen found it and carried it to Terpander and he took it to Egypt.[157]

In the Orphico-Pythagorean milieu, *mousike, mantike* and *iatrike* (music, divination and medicine) are united in the contemplative harmony of the "yoking" and "joining" succession

---

155. *Ibid.*, p. 182.

156. *The Manual of Harmonics of Nicomachus the Pythagorean*, tr. Flora R. Levin (Grand Rapids: Phanes Press, 1994), p. 189.

157. *Ibid.*

of order—in Sanskrit terms, *yoga* and *yuj*—that "describe the harmonic connection of string to instrument" and "the weapon's changing harmonic states".[158]

XVI

The extension of Ananke's arms throughout the entire universe is like the vastness of Nut-Hathor's cosmic body. In one of the numerous late Orphic cosmogonies, the golden chain derived from an allegorical interpretation of *Iliad* 8.19 illustrates the divine unity of the cosmos. Zeus himself suffuses all things and makes them one. As a short but impressive verse of the Orphic theological hymn testifies: "One Zeus, one Hades, one Helios, one Dionysus."[159]

Damascius cites Linus (the mythical singer and hierophant, presumed to be the son of the Muse Ourania) and Pythagoras "for the doctrine that everything is one".[160] The lament of Linus' poem, as it is quoted by Stobaeus, runs as follows:

> So through discord all things are steered through all. From
>   the whole are all things, all things from a whole, all things
>   are one, each part of all, all in one;
> For from a single whole all these things came,
> And from them in due time will one return,
> That's ever one and many. . . .
> Often the same will be again, no end will limit them, ever
>   limited. . . .
> For so undying death invests all things,
> All dies that's mortal, but the substrate was
> And is immortal ever, fashioned thus,

158. John Curtis Franklin, *Harmony in Greek and Indo-Iranian Cosmology*, p. 8.
159. M.L. West, *The Orphic Poems*, p. 253.
160. *Ibid.*, p. 61.

Yet with strange images and varied form
Will change and vanish from the sight of all.[161]

Some Orphic theological narratives and "holy oracles" of Night provide a mythical prototype for the philosophical vision of Parmenides and Empedocles. But Plato is scarcely concerned to do justice to Orpheus and other ancient "theologians", such as Musaeus and Epimenides, "who derive everything from Night".[162]

Since the ultimate limit is akin to limitless transcendence, the darkness of the Orphic Night and the primaeval ocean of the Heliopolitan theogony are symbolic descriptions of what is supra-noetic, ineffable, formless and unstructured, out of which the light-like noetic structure appears as the archetypal triad of Atum, Shu and Tefnut. According to Egyptian traditional accounts, "the world emerges from a primeval darkness (*keku semau*) and a primeval flood (*nun*). . . . In sum, the monotheism of the Egyptians consists in the belief that in the beginning the divine was one, and that in the cosmogony that was the work of the one, the one became many."[163]

It seems that Plato, as the dialectician of the one and the many, is just taking what he wants from Orpheus and certain limited Egyptian sources. Although Plato's dependence on the Night's prophets and Phanes' "logicians" is deliberately concealed, Plato's main philosophical doctrine is based on that of Parmenides; and Parmenides himself, in fact, depends on the Orphic myth. Even more, Parmenides (as a priest involved in the service of Apollo) and also the entire Velian school of philosophy, which is "plainly rooted in mysticism—it is rooted, in fact, in Parmenides' own chariot-experience, which leads . . . to the great Goddess' epiphany."[164]

---

161. *Ibid.*, p. 57.
162. *Ibid.*, p. 116.
163. Erik Hornung, *Idea into Image*, pp. 40 & 45.
164. Carl Levenson, *Socrates among the Coribantes: Being, Reality, and the Gods* (Woodstock, Connecticut: Spring Publications, 1999), p. 69.

The chariot journey may be a literary and telestic *topos*, of course, but this kind of metaphysical ascent (*anagoge*) is, moreover, the powerful symbol of a real dialectical alchemy, and serves as a paradigm of the divine revelation genre. Therefore, it comes as no surprise that Parmenides' description of Being as one and continuous is analogous to the Orphic theological myth, according to which the entire universe is united in the body of Zeus, "the only one", in the sense of the Theban Amun, the invisible solitary One who manifests "millions of visible embodiments" by his breath of life.

Likewise, Empedocles has his poetic, prophetic and theological precursor in Parmenides, the sky-walker whose chariot journey takes him into the House of Night. This *nuktos oikia* is the ineffable darkness from which Phanes emerges as a chariot-driving Sun, flying on its noetic wings. At the same time, it is the oracular sanctum, because Phanes himself bestowed the power of prophecy upon the primaeval Night.[165]

However, Night remains a source of wisdom and knowledge for all the universal rulers who follow her in the genealogical chain of theogony. In fact, this mythology of succession and violence is crowned by the episode in which Zeus swallows Phanes (the totality of the noetic archetypes) and thereby becomes the "beginning, middle and end of all". This myth is turned into "the philosophic basis for a monistic account of the genesis and governance of the world".[166]

In this particular context "Titanic" means "manifold", according to Velvet Yates, because it is precisely the Titans, as the principle of separation, who are made responsible for the world of plurality, for "creating the Many from the One".[167] Yates writes:

---

165. M.L. West, *The Orphic Poems*, p. 235.

166. Larry J. Alderink, *Creation and Salvation in Ancient Orphism* (Atlanta: Scholars Press, 1981), p. 53.

167. Velvet Yates, "The Titanic Origin of Humans: The Melian Nymphs and Zagreus," in *Greek, Roman, and Byzantine Studies* 44, 2004, p. 191.

On the cosmic level, the devouring of Dionysus' limbs by the Titans represents the generation of the material Many from the immaterial One. Proclus equates the division of Dionysus' body into seven parts by the Titans with the Timaeus' division of the world-soul into seven parts. At the human level, the Zagreus myth explains the fragmented nature of human thought. The Titans can also represent the forces of separation and fragmentation on the level of the individual soul. . . . [168]

This fragmentation and the subsequent forgetfulness only increase as the cosmic cycle evolves. Similarly in Egypt, Atum as the undifferentiated One in the transcendent darkness of Nun "comes into being by himself" (*kheper djesef*) and is turned (while essentially remaining the same) first into the Triad and then into the Ennead. In this way, the Egyptian scribes, like the later Neoplatonic dialecticians, unfolded a series of entities (at once numbers, symbols and iconographically fixed figures) that illustrates the unfolding of the paradigmatic structure of reality (conceived in the form of the decad) from its ultimate source in the One. According to the Pythagorean manual produced in the school of Iamblichus:

> Both Orpheus and Pythagoras made a particular point of describing the ennead as "pertaining to the Curetes", on the grounds that the rites sacred to the Curetes are tripartite, with three rites in each part, or as "Kore": both of these titles are appropriate to the triad, and the ennead contains the triad three times.[169]

The number nine thus expresses the paradigmatic, all-encompassing and still noetic totality. Put otherwise, the One

---

168. *Ibid.*, pp. 192-93.
169. *The Theology of Arithmetic: On the Mystical, Mathematical and Cosmological Symbolism of the First Ten Numbers, Attributed to Iamblichus*, tr. Robin Waterfield (Grand Rapids: Phanes Press, 1988), p. 107.

still belongs to the realm of the ineffable supra-noetic transcendence, but the goddess Neith (equated by the Platonists to Athena, the mistress of philosophy) calls the world of manifestation (*kheperu*) into being "through seven statements, which in a later magic text become the sevenfold laugh of the creator god".[170]

Mankind originated from Atum-Ra's tears, "in a temporary blurring" of Atum's vision, though the period of the golden age is still regarded as the solar kingdom of Ra, where gods and humans inhabit the stage of the extended sacred mound of Heliopolis together. During this blessed time (*paaut*)—before the human revolt against Ra—the divine *maat* (truth, perfect harmonious order) reigns.

XVII

In Platonic parlance, the main "initiatory" and "philosophical" goal of fallen humanity consists in the recollection of an ideal beginning and in solar contemplation of the enneadic totality of the Ideas. In order to do so, and achieve the desired goal, writing is established by Thoth and Sesheta as the instrument of revelation which provides access to the world of the gods; this is simply because it is, at the same time, the instrument of theophany and creation. In fact, the hieroglyphs (*medu neter*) are viewed as traces of noetic being, as archetypes and metaphysical symbols, even epiphanies of the gods themselves. They constitute the revealed body of divine knowledge necessary for salvation.[171]

After Ra's departure and the subsequent end of the direct divine rule, the distorted human race lives in a state of punishment and blindness. Hornung describes this as follows:

---

170. Erik Hornung, *Idea into Image*, p. 44.
171. Dimitri Meeks and Christine Favard-Meeks, *Daily Life of the Egyptian Gods*, tr. G. M. Goshgarian (London: John Murray, 1997), pp. 5-7.

Henceforth war and violence shape the lives of human beings. Having lost the paradisiacal innocence of their beginnings, they can regain access to the world of the gods only in death. Moreover, their rebellion suggests a dangerous threat to the continued existence of creation itself, insofar as it hints at the existence of destructive forces that seek to bring the normal course of events on earth to a halt.[172]

The memory of the divine presence is maintained by means of the Horus-like pharaoh whose rites enacted in the temple recall the initial foundation of the world as "revelation of the divine Face". The ritual act of unveiling and adoration of the Face establishes the royal paradigm of pious contemplation.

The Egyptians, in order to become a "holy people" once again, needed to walk "on the water of God", that is, follow the path of the deity (be it Atum-Ra, Amun-Ra, Ptah, Khnum or Sobek), proclaiming God's power even to the fish and the birds. This manifestation of divine power is to be regarded as a kind of revelation, as a miracle to be proclaimed, according to Assmann, so that the whole universe is told of the power of God.[173]

This all-encompassing proclamation of social *maat* practice, recollection and revelation, means that the ideal person is one who "is able to remember".[174] Accordingly, the ritual of the judgement of the dead assumes a kind of manual for the life-style and education of the living. The Egyptian initiate hopes "to go forth" and "to see Ra", ritually maintaining the metaphysical memory that conveys the pattern of alchemical transformation as well as rational calculability, responsibility and accountability. In this context the "initiate" simply means the official member of the pharaonic state who is able

---

172. Erik Hornung, *Idea into Image*, p. 48.
173. Jan Assmann, "Confession in Ancient Egypt," in *Transformations of the Inner Self in Ancient Religions*, ed. Jan Assmann and Guy G. Stroumsa (Leiden: Brill, 1999), p. 236.
174. *Ibid.*, p. 240.

to manage and present himself as a substitute (albeit inward-ly and mystically) for the king—either ideally patterned as Horus' image, or as the "mummified" and reanimated Osiris image. Finally, through the restored *akh*-identity, he hopes to be like a living god and stand in the sun barque.

Although the standard New Kingdom Egyptian is a po-litically responsible devotee of Amun and does not feel like a gnostic stranger in this world, death (*mut*) and initiation through the Osirian suffering and rebirth seems to be his only gateway to the noetic realm of Ra. Assmann argues that the gods are to be confronted "only by priests, indirectly in a statue ritual or directly after death",[175] when the Egyptian in the form of his *ba* appeals to the court of Osiris for justice:

> He does not accuse the gods for his misfortune, nor does he perceive his sufferings as unjust punishments for crimes he did not commit. He knows that the gods do not interfere in human affairs, and that a human being is exposed to all kinds of misfortunes that have nothing to do with the gods and have no religious significance whatsoever. They just occur. The only way to address the gods and to enter into forms of belonging and connectivity that bind him to the gods is to die and to present himself to the judgement of the dead.[176]

Proclus provides the following account, which presents an analogous but different story of royal succession and cyclic regression, based on the myth of the Titanic act of violence. Here the dismemberment of Dionysus (that partly follows the Osirian pattern) represents the proceeding of the One into the Many. Proclus says:

175. Jan Assmann, "A Dialogue Between Self and Soul: Papyrus Berlin 3024," in *Self, Soul and Body in Religious Experience*, ed. Albert I. Baumgarten with Jan Assmann and Guy G. Stroumsa (Leiden: Brill, 1998), p. 388.
176. *Ibid.*, pp. 400-01.

Orpheus the theologian had handed down three races of man: first the golden, which he says Phanes governed; second the silver, which he says the mighty Kronos ruled; third the Titanic, which he says Zeus assembled from the Titanic limbs; thinking that in these three categories every form of human life was included (*In Remp.* II.74-75; *Orph.frag.* 140).[177]

Yet another version is presented in the so-called *Rhapsodic Theogony* (the *Hieroi Logoi in 24 Rhapsodies*). In a related prayer to Apollo-Helios (at the beginning of the Orphic Rhapsodies) this poem is described as the twelfth revelation of Orpheus.[178] According to this Orphic theogony, current among the late Neoplatonists (especially Proclus, Damascius and Olympiodorus), there were six successive divine kingdoms ruled by Phanes, Night, Uranos, Kronos, Zeus and Dionysus respectively. Phanes reigns before Night in this account, and his reign (understood both metaphysically and as a pedagogical myth of perfect *politeia*) is somewhat analogous to the reign of Ra. Dionysus corresponds to Osiris, who comes back to life at the level of *anima mundi*—not only as the ruler of Duat (the Netherworld, tantamount to his own, or Nut-Hathor's, body-temple), but also as a model for the deceased, that is, for the "initiate" and "philosopher".

The main difference between the Egyptian and the Hellenic models is that the attainment of life (*ankh*) in the noetic Heliopolis depends not only upon knowledge and piety, but (first of all) upon service to the Egyptian holy state and to the pharaoh, the son of Ra, suckled by the goddess Hathor.[179] In the form of the *ka*-statue, located within the special mansions (wrongly designated as "mortuary temples" by modern scholars), he is expected to spend "millions of years" in

---

177. Velvet Yates, *The Titanic Origin of Humans: The Melian Nymphs and Zagreus*, p. 194.

178. M.L. West, *The Orphic Poems*, p. 227.

179. Dietrich Wildung, *Egyptian Saints: Deification in Pharaonic Egypt* (New York: New York University Press, 1977), p. 20.

mystic union with the deity.[180] His mummy (the symbolic image of Osiris) is the exemplary receiver of life (*shesep rankh*), of the reviving solar rays, thus becoming "his hieroglyphic spell generating his immortality",[181] and showing the theurgic way to his "initiates"—the bureaucratic and priestly staff. In this respect, he is the death-conquering immortal Horus, the golden Falcon. As Alan Segal remarks: "Eventually, ordinary Egyptians understood themselves and the transcendent part of their lives, by imitating the Pharaoh's path through the underworld. The afterlife became the mirror of the self."[182]

Since "the true and eternal life" begins (or rather, is regained) only with death, the term *ankhu*, "the living ones", as Gerhard Haeny aptly surmises, is used in a double sense: "of those alive on earth as well as of those living in the hereafter".[183]

XVIII

The language of Plato describing the Forms is reminiscent of the Parmenidean and Orphic revelations. This is not presumably an anachronistic "Platonic" reading of Parmenides, as certain modern historians of Hellenic philosophy would claim. Parmenides' otherworldly journey to the point where all the opposites meet, or are transcended, repeats that of Heracles and Orpheus. According to Kingsley: "Everyone runs from death so everyone runs away from wisdom. . . . Parmenides' journey takes him in exactly the opposite direction. . . . To

---

180. Gerhard Haeny, "New Kingdom 'Mortuary Temples' and 'Mansions of Millions of Years,'" in *Temples of Ancient Egypt*, ed. Byron E. Shafer (London: I. B. Tauris, 1998), p. 86.

181. Alan F. Segal, *Life after Death: A History of the Afterlife in Western Religion* (New York: Doubleday, 2004), p. 50.

182. *Ibid.*, p. 69.

183. Gerhard Haeny, *ibid.*, p. 92.

die before you die, no longer to live on the surface of yourself: this is what Parmenides is pointing to."[184]

It is no surprise that Parmenides articulated the epistemological and ontological categories fundamental to Platonism. The deliberately pro-Platonic understanding of Parmenides' "unmoving heart of well-rounded Truth" (*aletheies eukukleos atremes etor*: I.29)[185] was common among later Platonists. Therefore, Plato's actual reception of Parmenides must itself be important for an historically relevant interpretation of the Parmenides poem, a reception indicated by the *Phaedrus* myth and Plato's comparison of the soul to a charioteer with a pair of winged horses, not unlike the horses of Phanes "conveyed here and there by golden wings" (Hermeias, *In Phaedr.* 142.13 ff; *Orph. Frag.* 78). According to John Palmer, Hermeias properly connected Plato's image of the chariot with analogous images used by Orpheus and Parmenides. He criticises Leonardo Taran's assertion, namely, that in Parmenides nothing suggests the comparison of the chariot with the soul, as absurd, saying: "Suggests to whom? Certainly not to one who would have recognized, for example, the parallels between the proem and Orphic accounts of the initiate's experience of the afterlife."[186]

Regarding Plato's description of the Forms in Parmenidean language, Palmer argues that both the *Phaedrus* and the *Republic* myths incorporate certain Parmenidean and Orphic elements into the context of a revelation of pure Being that repeats the revelation received in Parmenides's *anabasis*:

Each revelation in the *Republic* takes place only after the soul's journey to an ouranian (possibly hyperouranian) re-

184. Peter Kingsley, *In the Dark Places of Wisdom* (Inverness, CA: The Golden Sufi Center, 1999), pp. 64-65.

185. Raymond Adolph Prier, *Archaic Logic: Symbol and Structure in Heraklitus, Parmenides, and Empedocles* (The Hague: Mouton, 1976), p. 97.

186. John A. Palmer, *Plato's Reception of Parmenides* (Oxford: Clarendon Press, 1999), p. 18.

gion. If either is supposed to have a Parmenidean analogue—
that is, if the myth of Er does indeed draw upon Parmenides—then . . . it implies an interpretation of the proem as
ascent. . . . Because of the presence in the proem of imagery
of the Orphic initiate's post-mortem experience as described
in the verses on the gold lamellae . . . it would be straightfor-
ward for Plato to interpret the proem as Parmenides' account
of his own afterlife experience (or something analogous to
it such as a dream). The connections between Parmenides'
proem and Plato's myths are unlikely to be merely a function
of their having a common source in Orphic and Pythagorean
eschatology. . . . Parmenides would have seemed unique in
providing a model for both the content and the conditions of
the unfettered soul's vision of Being. The theoretical compo-
nent of this post-mortem vision is . . . Plato's view that learning essentially involves a process of recollection. The symbio-
sis between the recollection theory and the revelation theme
is clearest at *Phaedrus* 249b6-c4. . . . [187]

Indeed, for Plato, "learning is nothing but recollection"
(*mathesis ouk allo ti e anamnesis. . . . Phaed.* 72e5-6), and this
recollection constitutes a non-propositional and non-repre-
sentational knowledge of the Forms. Presumably, this knowledge is infallible, and belongs to the ideal knowers, likened to
gods. Such knowers enter the "divine constellation" either by
means of dialectic, the performance of ritual, or after death.
The process of mystagogy (education imagined as recollection) is like a dialogue between "the-one-who-loves-knowledge" and a deity, "He-who-praises-knowledge" (and, in fact,
reveals knowledge), namely, Thoth in the Late Period Egyptian *Book of Thoth*.[188]

187. *Ibid.*, pp. 22-23.
188. Richard Jasnow and Karl-Theodor Zauzich, *The Ancient Egyptian Book of Thoth: A Demotic Discourse on Knowledge and Pendant to the Classical Hermetica. Volume 1: Text* (Wiesbaden: Harrassowitz Verlag, 2005), p. 3.

The Parmenidean and Platonic lover of knowledge is akin to the divine and immortal Being, thus reaffirming the "truest nature of the soul". Only the qualified Platonic *philosophos* is purified to such a degree that he achieves what others do not, namely, the realisation of his affinity (*sungenes*) with the divine. Consequently, by becoming real knowers—that is, by imitating (*mimeisthai*) the Forms and making themselves likenesses of them—philosophers become akin to the noetic Forms.[189] Or put otherwise, they become like the eternal hieroglyphs in the form of *akhu*.

As Gerson explains, "the person achieves his true nature in knowing Forms"; and this person is not a human being, because the human body does not belong ideally to one's identity. Only by acquiring knowledge does the righteous "dead man" acquire a new identity, because knowledge entails self-transformation.[190] And this desired identity is a noetic or divine identity of sorts.

However, if philosophy is nothing but a practice for dying and being dead (*Phaed.* 64a.5-6; 67d.7-10), then philosophy, in its initial purificatory phase at least, is the Osirian way of life, in spite of any reluctance to acknowledge the theological identity of Osiris and Dionysus. And Orpheus may be called "the first philosopher" (as Diogenes Laertius asserts and questions: *Vitae* I.5), but only in the same metaphorical and thoroughly "sloganised" sense in which Imhotep, the son of Ptah, "successful in his actions, great in miracles", is "the first philosopher" of the Egyptians.

The Platonic myth (*muthos*) which, presumably, "represents philosophy's culmination",[191] is the Orphico-Pythagorean soteriological manifesto. For according to Plato, the souls of pious philosopher-gnostics (the knowers of Ideas, or Forms) are purified of the mortal body and thereby join the

---

189. Lloyd P. Gerson, *Knowing Persons: A Study in Plato*, pp. 128-29.
190. *Ibid.*, p. 115.
191. Kathryn A. Morgan, *Myth and Philosophy from the Presocratics to Plato*, p. 185.

immortal gods. Philosophers are destined for the Isles of the Blest, therefore Socrates considers it most fitting for those who are about to make the otherworldly journey "to examine and mythologise" (*diaskopein te kai muthologein*) about it (*Phaedr.* 61e1-3).[192]

XIX

Human learning may be contrasted to the divine omniscience as discursive reasoning is to Neoplatonic intellection (*noesis*). The first is a sort of dialectic which uses classifying division and collection, and strives for rational "scientific knowledge"; the second a kind of non-discursive dialectic which rules out not only transition from subject to predicate, but even language itself, and which noerically contemplates and apprehends all that is as a *totum simul*.[193]

This *noesis* is something more than the type of rational or intellectual activity capable of producing coherent texts, systems and interpretations, because it implies the soul's identity (or affinity with) *ta noeta* (the Forms). Such identity at the level of *Nous* may be designated as salvation achieved either by the unity of soul and intellect, or by "the reflection in the logical soul of *noeseis* in the form of *ennoiai*",[194] that is, in the form of illuminating thoughts and mystical insights.

The main driving force of Platonic *paideia* is not simply a one-sided *logos*, but the god-given *eros*, that is, one's striving for unification with the supreme *arche* and the desire of noetic immortality through the *daimon* that God has given to each of us. Plato says: "And so far as it is possible for human nature to have a share in immortality, he will not in any degree lack

192. *Ibid.*, p. 194.
193. A.C. Lloyd, *The Anatomy of Neoplatonism* (Oxford: Clarendon Press, 1991), p. 165.
194. Andrew Smith, *Porphyry's Place in the Neoplatonic Tradition: A Study in Post-Plotinian Neoplatonism* (The Hague: Martinus Nijhoff, 1974), p. 53.

this. And because he always takes care of that which is divine, and has the *daimon* that lives with him well ordered (*eu keko-smemenon*), he will be supremely happy (*eudaimon*)" (*Theaet.* 90c). Gregory Vlastos therefore connects Plato's theory of love with his "religious mysticism", arguing that the convergence of *mania* and *nous* in love shows Plato's affinity to the "orgiastic Dionysian rites".[195]

Since the embodied soul is "dismembered" and "scattered" like Osiris, its recollection, restoration and ascent to the One by means of *Nous* is related to the soul's going "out of its mind drunk with the nectar", as Plotinus would say (*Enn.* VI.7.35.25-26), that is, out of its discursive *logismos*. Therefore Shaw concludes that rational thinking for Plato "has a purely cathartic function", because the soul's purification and the subsequent restoration of its lost divinity "was the way of Platonic *paideia*, and while a well-exercised skill in rational analysis was necessary to strip the soul of false beliefs, it could never awaken it to its innate dignity."[196]

This teaching of philosophical *katharsis* as a way of release from the wheel of rebirth and entry to everlasting noetic bliss—the privilege of ruling the whole cosmos with the gods (moving in the barque of Ra or following the chariot of Zeus)—is based on "a religious doctrine, which Plato took over from Orphics or Pythagoreans, a doctrine of sin, purgatory, reincarnation, and eventual purification", according to David Bostock.[197]

Therefore, the Platonic learning itinerary follows the eternal standards (*paradeigmata*) established in divine reality, and consequently associates the ideal of contemplating (*theorein*) with that of serving or "caring for" (*therapeuein*) the divini-

---

195. Gregory Vlastos, "The Individual as an Object of Love in Plato," in *Plato*, ed. Gail Fine (Oxford: Oxford University Press, 2000), pp. 638-39.
196. Gregory Shaw, "After Aporia: Theurgy in Later Platonism," in *The Journal of Neoplatonic Studies*, vol. V, no.1, Fall 1996, pp. 5-6.
197. David Bostock, "The Soul and Immortality in Plato's Phaedo," in *Plato*, ed. Gail Fine (Oxford: Oxford University Press, 2000), p. 893.

ty.[198] Since God is the measure of all things and the standard for justice, to become like God, for Plato, means to become just, holy (*hosiotes*) and wise, for he says: "And that is why we should also try to escape from here to there as quickly as we can. To escape is to become like god so far as it is possible (*phuge de homoiosis theoi kata to dunaton*), and to become like god is to become just and holy, together with wisdom" (*Theaet.* 176a).[199]

The erotic pathway to wisdom is presented by the priestess Diotima (whose name means "honour of god") of Mantinea (related to *mantis*, "prophet" or "seer").[200] Her task as the ideal Platonic mystagogue is to destroy the initiate's constructed "old self" following the Orphic spiritual method: "No ideology could survive Diotima's scrutiny," as Rappe observes: "mind and body arise together as mutually conditioned constructions. Self-identity ebbs away in the flow of memory while consciousness disappears without a trace of its previous contents."[201] The lover of wisdom in his upward movement hopes to participate in the absolute Beauty (*metechei ekeinou tou kalou*), and not simply arrive at a "clear definition" by using division (*diairesis*) and collection (*sunagoge*) in the manner of a priest dissecting a sacrificial animal (*hoion hiereion*: *Soph.* 287c3).[202]

The soul of the dialectician is able "to see the truth" (*aletheia horatai*: *Rep.* 527c3) only when it reaches the "limit of the intelligible" (*tou noetou telei*: *Rep.* 532b2). However, the dialectical procedure of "exhaustive classification" carried out by tortuous division, collection and definition is viewed

---

198. David Sedley, "The Ideal of Godlikeness," in *Plato*, ed. Gail Fine (Oxford: Oxford University Press, 2000), p. 810.

199. *Ibid.*, p. 794.

200. Kenneth M. Sayre, *Plato's Literary Garden: How to Read a Platonic Dialogue* (Notre Dame and London: University of Notre Dame Press, 1995), p. 108.

201. Sara Rappe, *Reading Neoplatonism: Non-discursive Thinking in the Texts of Plotinus, Proclus, and Damascius*, p. 152.

202. Kenneth M. Sayre, *ibid.*, p. 149.

as a divinely revealed path (*hodos*), that is, as a "gift from the gods to men" (*Phileb.* 16c5; 16b5; 16a8).²⁰³ According to Plato, one can never gain knowledge (*episteme*, not merely opinion) by simply reasoning about something, because one needs to be "enamoured" by the "godly method". In short, one needs some kind of inducement in order to turn "the eye of the soul" (*Rep.* 540a7) upward towards the final revelation of the Beautiful and the Good.

Kenneth Sayre argues that the philosophical goal to be achieved cannot be reached simply by taking certain steps in that direction, because the Platonic *methodos* has nothing to do with "a routine procedure for cranking out certain results, like the method of long division in arithmetic".²⁰⁴ He explains:

> The Greek term *methodos* comes from *hodos* (way) plus *meta* (in the sense of "according to"), so that a *methodos* literally is a path or a way that one might pursue to a given goal. . . . Plato's term *dialektike*, after all, is a derivative of the verb *dialegomai*, meaning to converse with another person. And the manner of conversation in question is one in which the master philosopher directs the steps of the relative neophyte.²⁰⁵

XX

The Egyptian term *sia* is difficult to render. However, Dimitri Meeks and Christine Favard-Meeks maintain that it designates the special noetic faculty "that enabled the gods to perceive an event the instant it occurred, together with the reason for its occurrence".²⁰⁶ Being thus equivalent to noetic il-

---

203. *Ibid.*, p. 150.
204. *Ibid.*, p. 160.
205. *Ibid.*, pp. 160 & 161.
206. Dimitri Meeks and Christine Favard-Meeks, *Daily Life of the Egyptians Gods*, p. 95.

lumination and all-embracing *gnosis, sia* presumably includes all possible knowledge, and is found in Atum-Ra's shining Eye as its universal irradiation. In a pair with Hu (the creative utterance), the personified Sia (sometimes interpreted as meaning "perception") stands in the solar barque of Ra:

> This capacity, which every god possessed in some measure, was a dormant kind of knowledge that became active in the presence of the event that brought it out; it enabled a god to grasp, in the fullest sense of the word, what was going on. It made it possible for already existing knowledge, reactivated by a signal, to emerge at the conscious level. "Sign of recognition", that is the basic meaning of the word *sia* in Egyptian. . . . Thus was established a rather clear-cut distinction between *sia*, or synthetic knowledge, and knowledge as technique and praxis, called *rekh*. *Sia* operated like an absolute intuition irreducible to logical knowledge. *Rekh* implied a way of defining concepts that necessarily entailed the use of speech, and, later, writing; they endowed it with . . . the capacity to be transmitted.[207]

However, one cannot be sure that the term *rekh* simply means something like discursive or scientific-encyclopaedic knowledge. In many contexts, *rekh* is an equivalent of the initiatory gnosis necessary for the successful arrival at "the shore of the great island", namely, the divine realm, and for appearing as a god.

The disciple to whom the god of wisdom reveals different types of useful scribal, theological and scholarly knowledge in the Egyptian demotic *Book of Thoth* is the "lover of wisdom" (*mer-rekh*), that is, the "philosopher" in its original Pythagorean sense.

Richard Jasnow and Karl-Theodor Zauzich argue that the role of the *mer-rekh* "raises the problem of initiation and mysticism", because among the goals of the *mer-rekh* are partici-

---

207. *Ibid.*, pp. 95-96.

pation in alchemical transformations (liturgies, rituals, her-meneutical events) in the Duat and eventually joining Ra in his solar barque. They say:

> We know of no examples of this striking Egyptian parallel to Greek *Philosophos* outside of the Book of Thoth. . . . *Mer-rekh* designates the aspiring student or scholar who desires to be initiated into the wisdom of Thoth. . . . His relationship with the deities is a close one; Thoth treats him virtually as a son. . . . [208]

The dialogue between the The-one-of-Heseret (Thoth) and the *mer-rekh* is modelled on an initiatory underworld dialogue employed in the literature of the New Kingdom. The Platonic dialogues follow this pattern. Though the demotic Book of Thoth itself is perhaps later than Plato, its patterns and ideas are based on the Ramesside theological *rekh*.

In the context of priestly mystagogy, Imhotep (the chief lector-priest of Heliopolis) was regarded as an ideal sage or bearer of knowledge (*rekh-ikhet*). He is a paradigm for every subsequent Egyptian *philosophos*, since, though designated as the son of Ptah, he was a mortal man whose *ba* ascend-ed to heaven and became a god. Consequently, Imhotep is the model for the initiatory death and transformation which every *mer-rekh* hopes to accomplish.[209] As Hornung plainly states, there is a constant "gnostic" stress on knowledge (most frequently secret knowledge), "through which alone, in good Egyptian tradition, salvation and redemption is achieved".[210]

The dialectical action of the Book of Thoth (which survives in damaged fragments) probably is set in the mandala-like

208. Richard Jasnow and Karl-Theodor Zauzich, *The Ancient Egyptian Book of Thoth: A Demotic Discourse on Knowledge and Pendant to the Classical Hermetica. Volume 1: Text*, p. 13.

209. *Ibid.*, p. 19.

210. Erik Hornung, *The Secret Lore of Egypt: Its Impact on the West*, tr. David Lorton (Ithaca and London: Cornell University Press, 2001), p. 44.

House of Life (*per ankh*) and dramatised in connection with divine festivals (a connection also suggested by the dramatic setting of certain Platonic dialogues). Jasnow and Zauzich write:

> There is little doubt that the constituent elements of the House of Life could be imbued with symbolic force; the author may conceive this institution as reflecting the underworld or, perhaps better, the divine world. Similarly, the author of the Book of Thoth may sometimes employ metaphorical language. The process of attaining mastery of scribal knowledge, for example, may mirror the deceased's striving to attain rebirth. . . . Thereupon the *mer-rekh* praises Thoth for his advice, and expresses his own hopes for what amounts almost to a spiritual rebirth. . . . The *mer-rekh* offers a recitation of praise to Thoth or Imhotep at the festival of Imhotep. He expresses the wish to join his entourage, become a seer, and worship Seshat. The *mer-rekh* further proclaims personal experience and knowledge of such events as Thoth's defeat of the enemies of Ra in the underworld. . . . He introduces himself, answering the question: "Who are you?" with the words: "I am the *mer-rekh*."[211]

Hence, he is the "lover of wisdom", and wisdom is embodied by Thoth to whom he avows his loyalty, showing desire to worship this god, partake in his rituals and processions, and understand their hidden symbolic meaning. It seems that the ideal *mer-rekh* is a pious scribe or scholar, sometimes functioning as the lector priest, like Imhotep. In accordance with the chief theological paradigm, he enters the barque of Ra, thus being like the transfigured *akh*, and not the material corpse (*mut*). He is both "prophet" and "craftsman", the servant of Thoth and other gods, including Ptah.

---

211. Richard Jasnow and Karl-Theodor Zauzich, *ibid.*, pp. 3, 6 & 8. (The transliteration of some Egyptian words is slightly altered, for example *mr-rh* became *mer-rekh* in order to make it more readable.)

In this respect, "the-one-who-loves-knowledge" (*mer-rekh*) is analogous to the great Imhotep or Amenhotep, Son-of-Hapu. The Egyptian scribes and religious scholars, those concerned with the sacred books—"manifestations of Ra" (*bau Ra*)—hope "to be united with Amenhotep and Imhotep in the afterlife".[212]

The holy "books" (the hieroglyphic and hieratic compositions of texts and symbolic pictures, as well as statues, reliefs, sanctuaries and tombs) are solar in their essential nature. Therefore, the "souls of Ra" (*bau Ra*) may be depicted as constituting the crew in the barque of Ra. Thereby the close relationship between prophecy and writing is assumed and emphasised.

The Egyptian verb *ser* means to show, to announce, hence, to prophesy. When the *mer-rekh* receives instructions from "He-who-praises-knowledge" (Thoth), the "prophecy" virtually becomes revelation and reception of "philosophy" (using this word in its strictly etymological sense as the "love of wisdom").

The lord of the *bau* of Ra is the messenger of prophecy, and the servant of Thoth is a receiver of prophecy brought by Thoth. Therefore, the *mer-rekh* is also the writer and the reciter, following the standard request for revelation and the divine command to recite (somewhat resembling the Quranic command): "Come you, O one who lives as the craftsman of Isten. O praised one of the heart of Ra, may he cause that you recite."[213]

The Book of Thoth speaks of the chamber of Darkness, and mentions "a lamp of prophecy". Moreover, its dialogues may be staged as an initiatory drama, performed by priestly actors. The *mer-rekh* is frequently designated as a "youth" (*nekhen*), analogous to the Hellenic Apollonian *kouros* or the Arabic *fata*. He hopes to participate in rituals of the divine

212. Dietrich Wildung, *Egyptian Saints: Deification in Pharaonic Egypt*, p. 105.
213. Richard Jasnow and Karl-Theodor Zauzich, *ibid.*, p. 32.

realm, to become the "blessed deceased" in the entourage of Thoth and other gods, thereby stressing the secrets of his patron Thoth and the related knowledge of the Osirian Duat. Accordingly, the *mer-rekh* strives for spiritual rebirth.[214] Jasnow and Zauzich comment as follows:

> It does seem fair to say that in the Book of Thoth the *mer-rekh*, be he priest or student, undergoes a type of initiation and spiritual rebirth. The knowledge imparted is strongly, but not solely, underworldly in character. We believe that the process takes place while the *mer-rekh* is alive, within the context of the temple House of Life, and probably in connection with festivals. It is quite likely that in entering the sacred space of the temple and House of Life the participant was simultaneously conceived to be entering the underworld or, at least, the divine otherworld. . . . The disciple achieves a sort of rebirth, perhaps through the equivalent of the Opening of the Mouth Ceremony, which then results in his recitation of a hymn to Imhotep/Thoth. . . . *Rekh* prepares one's way into the Beyond.[215]

XXI

Robert Lamberton states that the inspired Orphic poetry had a privileged religious position from the time of Socrates and before, to the time of Damascius and holy Serapion, who "possessed and read almost nothing except the writings of Orpheus" (Damascius *Phil. Hist.* 111).[216] No wonder Orpheus

---

214. In this respect, see *Algis Uzdavinys, Philosophy as a Rite of Rebirth: From Ancient Egypt to Neoplatonism* (Westbury: The Prometheus Trust, 2008).

215. Richard Jasnow and Karl-Theodor Zauzich, *ibid.*, pp. 58, 59 & 62.

216. Robert Lamberton, "The Neoplatonists and their Books," in *Homer, the Bible, and Beyond: Literary and Religious Canons in the Ancient World*, ed. Margalit Finkelberg and Guy G. Stroumsa (Leiden: Brill, 2003), pp. 207 & 208; *Damascius: The Philosophical History*, text with translation and notes by Polymnia Athanassiadi (Athens: Apamea, 1999), p. 267.

was designated simply as "the Theologian", in much the same way as Homer was named "the Poet".[217]

Homer, as a privileged mythical *auctoritas*, supplied the Hellenes with the highly selective and largely spurious "sacred map" of Heroic Greece, thus deliberately shaping their collective memory and using a language "never spoken by any living person".[218] This modified picture of the heroic past and a shadowy afterlife, codified in sixth century BC Athens, provided the pattern of the initially aristocratic pan-Hellenic unity and the alleged "theological" continuity of their world view.

Of course, the Homeric poems were read as Pythagorean or Stoic philosophical allegories, and Proclus defended Homer by linking his poetry with the god Apollo and claiming that the Homeric poems remind us of transcendent things. In this case, "a symbolic mode of representation becomes a necessity."[219] Likewise, in the Egyptian tradition of ritual exegesis (followed by the Orphic "paradoxical and implausible interpretive strategies"[220]) everything related with cultic communication and mystagogy must be symbolic. According to Assmann:

> For nothing in the Egyptian cult is just what it appears to be. The priest is not a priest; the statue is not a statue; the sacrificial substances and requisites are not what they are usually. In the context of the ritual performance all acquire a special "mythical" meaning that points to something else in "yonder world". . . . Everything in this sacred game becomes a kind of hieroglyph. . . . The more there was to interpret, the more mysterious the rite became. The dialectics of interpreta-

---

217. Robert Lamberton, *ibid.*, p. 207.

218. Margalit Finkelberg, "Homer as a Foundation Text," in *Homer, the Bible, and Beyond: Literary and Religious Canons in the Ancient World*, ed. Margalit Finkelberg and Guy G. Stroumsa (Leiden: Brill, 2003), p. 207.

219. Oiva Kuisma, *Proclus' Defence of Homer* (Helsinki: Societies Scientiarum Fennica, 1996), p. 106.

220. Robert Lamberton, *The Neoplatonists and their Books*, p. 207.

tion and arcanization led to a cultural split between a surface structure of religious practices of sometimes appealing
absurdity . . . and a deep structure of religious philosophy,
which finally developed into hermetism, where the sacerdotal
science of Egyptian paganism and the philosophical religion
of neo-Platonism met to form the last stage of Egyptian religion.[221]

After the so-called Homeric age (or even simultaneous with
it), a radical shift had occurred in the ancient Greek mentality
as regards the understanding of the soul and its relation to
the body. This shift coincides with the so-called Saite renais-
sance in Egypt and the Egyptian "holy war"—using Greek
mercenaries—with Assyria. Precisely at this time, Egypt sys-
tematically turned to the models of the past, and this pious
codification of cultural standards according to the "eternal"
schemata is later reflected and made programmatic in Plato's
Laws. Assmann writes:

> Much more comprehensively than in the Ramesside age,
> Egypt now discovered its own antiquity and elevated it to the
> rank of a normative past. Almost the entire literate upper stra-
> tum—above all, the kings themselves—now began to emulate
> Prince Khaemwaset by visiting and copying the monuments
> of their forefathers. This wholesale return to the models of
> the past was tantamount to a cultural revolution and it spread
> into every aspect of Egyptian life.[222]

It therefore cannot be assumed that the people of Greece
suddenly and rather spontaneously started to question the
reliability of their traditional cosmology and anthropology,

---

221. Jan Assmann, *Semiosis and Interpretation in Ancient Egyptian Ritual*,
pp. 104 & 106.
222. Jan Assmann, *The Mind of Egypt: History and Meaning in the Time of
the Pharaohs*, tr. Andrew Jenkins (New York: Metropolitan Books, 2002),
p. 341.

making inquiries into "the metaphysical background of physical phenomena" and eventually discovering "a difference
between the corporeal and the spiritual aspects of life", as
Rein Ferwerda supposes.[223] However, all kinds of cultic associations were incorporated into the ritualised and interiorised
procedures of salvation in the attempt to release that part of
the person now called the "immortal soul" (*psuche*), following
(with the enthusiasm of recent converts) Egyptian theological and soteriological paradigms.

The road leading to Osiris Un-nefer trodden by the initiates in their hope that death is not akin to complete dis-
solution (leading simply to the lamentable condition of the
simulacrum of the body being lost) now became the "mystic
road to Rhadamanthus", marking the release of the soul from
the body. This separation from the ultimately devalued mortal body and subsequent transition may be somewhat ritually
anticipated, or even performed, by the mystical symbols of
the Dionysiac initiations (*ta mustika sumbola ton peri ton Dio-
nuson orgiasmon*). Hence, the Orphic golden tablet addresses
the deceased (the one who has died in either the philosophical or the physical sense, or one who is still in the process of
learning the eschatological rhetoric) as follows: "Happy and
blessed one, you will be a god instead of mortal" (*olbie kai
makariste, theos d'esei anti brotoio*).[224]

At first this Orphic teaching of *soteria* was a secret teaching
which, perhaps, would look too unconvincing and ridiculous
for the traditionally minded majority of Hellenes. The rhetoric of the "secrecy" was structured so that any "secret" (be
it just a pedagogical fiction) needed to be revealed, whilst

---

223. Rein Ferwerda, "The Meaning of the Word σῶμα (Body) in the Axial
Age: An Interpretation of Plato's CRATYLUS," in *The Origins and Diversity
of Axial Age Civilizations*, ed. S. N. Eisenstadt (Albany: State University of
New York Press, 1986), p. 112.

224. Susan Guettel Cole, "Voices from beyond the Grave: Dionysus and
the Dead," in *Masks of Dionysus*, ed. Thomas H. Carpenter and Christopher
A. Pharaone (Ithaca and London: Cornell University Press, 1993), p. 278.

at the same time maintaining the inadequacy of attempting to communicate in words the mystical essence of the *telete*, which is to be realised only by ritual participation.

In the context of establishing and keeping various practices and orders, the claims of secrecy do not consist in concealing some exclusive or dangerous knowledge, as the romantic Protestant "esoterism" of a nineteenth century Western mentality imagines in its obsession with "secret societies" and "inward experiences" of "genuine initiations". Rather it serves for the formation and maintainence of social boundaries. For the insiders, the established practices, signs of distinction and solemn slogans of "secrecy" must be preserved and transmitted in order for them to survive as a community of privileged truth-bearers.

It goes without saying that these groups which celebrated all sorts of festivals and practised telestic rites (that imitate festivals anyway) were neither the "secret societies" of Masonic fantasy, nor "esoteric centres" in the sense employed by the "universal" post-Hegelian theosophy of those who accept the crazy theory of secret forces of evil operating in history and plotting against the *verus Israel*. Accordingly, Luther Martin analyses the "syndrome of secrecy" in certain "textual communities", especially in relation to the Hermetic distinction between secret (unofficial, underground, forbidden) and public (official) knowledge. Due to this cultural schizophrenia (that unfolded between Athens and Jerusalem), the entire world theatre was transformed (following Egyptian and Babylonian scriptural paradigms) into the esoteric book, open to sectarian readings and rereadings. As Martin explains:

> Like secrecy, such literary productions create their alternative world, and such textual societies . . . reviled and rejected the external world which represented, from their perspective, a universe of diminished literacy beyond their own revelatory texts. They did not, however, fear this world like the local associations and oral cultures they replaced. Rather than cowering with the protective embrace of secret enclaves, the goal of such textual societies was nothing less than the militant

mastery and domination of the entire universe. . . . Christians, who had initially demonized a world of adversarial others . . . came to employ . . . exorcism to establish their own catholicity. . . . And when one of these cultic claims to an identifying revelation came to define the dominant and inclusive cultural reality, exclusivistic claims to sacrality became reimagined as the esoteric contents of traditions past. Occluded by a regnant Christianity, it is precisely the Hermetic and Gnostic heritage that produced for Western culture its "syndrome of the secret."[225]

XXII

The early Hellenic *teletai* (including the Orphic *bakcheia*) and the mysteries were officially recognised by the Athenian state and rearranged as the politically and socially significant rite of "civic eschatology" performed in Eleusis. According to Jan Bremmer, the Eleusinian Mysteries began to be used "for political aims by stressing their civilising function" and their religio-ideological power: "The First Fruits decree had made the Mysteries into the symbol of Athenian power *par exellence*. The revelation of its contents was a political act. . . . "[226]

Orpheus the Theologian was placed on the same firmly established foundation as Homer the Theologian. However, the mysteries in the form of various unspeakable or ineffable (*arrheta*) and secret or esoteric (*aporrheta*) *teletai*, "aimed at a change of mind through experience of the sacred" and salva-

---

225. Luther H. Martin, "Secrecy in Hellenistic Religious Communities," in *Secrecy and Concealment: Studies in the History of Mediterranean and Near Eastern Religions*, ed. Hans G. Kippenberg and Guy G. Stroumsa (Leiden: E. J. Brill, 1995), pp. 116 & 117.

226. Jan N. Bremmer, "Religious Secrets and Secrecy in Classical Greece," in Secrecy and Concealment: Studies in the History of Mediterranean and Near Eastern Religions, ed. Hans G. Kippenberg and Guy G. Stroumsa (Leiden: E.J. Brill, 1995), p. 75.

tion "through closeness to the divine",[227] depended on a private and personal decision and a vow.

To make an oath and be initiated into the *thiasos* (a remote antique prototype of the Sufi *tariqah*, likewise based on a relationship between a patron and his clients) is tantamount to making a covenant (or legal treaty) with a deity in the Neo-Assyrian and Biblical contexts. This is so because the divine saviour is regarded as the patron of the client who is to be saved. Consequently, the human royal patron and saviour may be called *theos epiphanes eucharistos*, as Ptolemy V of Egypt is designated (the hieroglyphic equivalents, according to Arthur Nock, being the god "who comes forth" and "lord of beauties").[228]

According to Burkert, charisma and the display of power override all other forms of reverential awe (*sebas*), because the attraction of the royal epiphany (like Amun's epiphany in New Kingdom Thebes) is overwhelming. Hence:

> The experience of "epiphany" came to concentrate on the person of the ruler who had acted as a "savior" and inaugurated an age of bliss and abundance—a process that easily assumed a Dionysiac coloring. . . . The monarch was the victor, the savior, the god, "present" (*epiphanes*) to a degree gods had hardly ever been. Not only the actors followed in his wake, but "all sorts of *thiasoi*", including those of *mustai* and *bakchoi*.[229]

Every professional association (*hetairia*) claimed the patronage of one or more deities, and was made up of the deities' servants, vassals and cult-worshippers. These societies

227. Walter Burkert, *Ancient Mystery Cults* (Cambridge MA: Harvard University Press, 1987), pp. 11-12.

228. Arthur Darby Nock, "Notes on Ruler-Cult, I-IV," *Essays on Religion and the Ancient World, Selected and edited, with an Introduction, Bibliography of Nock's writings, and Indexes, by Zeph Stewart, vol.1* (Oxford: Clarendon Press, 1986), p. 152 (p. 37).

229. Walter Burkert, *Bacchic Teletai in the Hellenistic Age*, p. 268.

were sometimes called *orgeones*, from *orgiazo*, "to pay ritual service to the gods", and their ritual practices were *ta orgia*. They usually included a banquet (*sumposion*) where the members of the *hetairia* or initiates sat crowned with garlands on sacred couches. In this way, the *stephanos* (wreath, garland) was worn by the "dead" initiate and the corpse alike. The participant of the earthly drinking party—playing the role of Dionysus restored or Osiris resurrected—imitated the "living one" of the heavenly symposium.

The ceremonial drinking and its established representational hierarchy brings the rulers and the royal initiates to the divine status of bliss, making them close to the gods.[230] Since the gods are no longer in fact *homotrapezoi*, "table companions" of men, and are to be addressed through ritual mediation,[231] the ceremonial banquet serves as a means to imitate (or play) the gods and thereby restore (symbolically, at least) perfect heavenly bliss.

According to Rappe, for the late Neoplatonists the dismemberment of Dionysus signified both a phase in the manifestation of the cosmos (in the sense of the Pythagorean numerical progression) and the setting of the stage for the soul's ultimate liberation and glorification at the noetic symposium. She explains:

> For Proclus, the Orphic theology, in offering a vision of the great world encompassed in the pleroma of the human intellect and embodied within the perfect person, Phanes, shows forth the soul as an *imago dei*. It is this recognition that in itself constitutes a form of initiation, making possible the soul's access to the fullness of reality. . . . Once more, the creative,

---

230. Walter Burkert, "Oriental Symposia: Contrasts and Parallels," in *Dining in a Classical Context*, ed. William J. Slater (Ann Arbor: University of Michigan Press, 1991), p. 8.

231. Philippe Borgeaud, "Melampous and Epimenides: Two Greek Paradigms of the Treatment of Mistake," in *Transformations of the Inner Self in Ancient Religions*, ed. Jan Assmann and Guy G. Stroumsa (Leiden: Brill, 1999), p. 288.

divine energy that pours itself through the various stations of being as stages within the theology is initiatory in function.[232]

Presumably, ritual initiation into the early Hellenic *hetairia* implied a pedagogical rather than a hidden or concealed relationship—and, consequently, one's preparation for the *a priori* established role of the "blessed initiate", and not a sort of miraculous transubstantiation.

As Martin emphasises, "initiation into the Eleusinian, as in the other mysteries, was equivalent to adoption by the presiding deity,"[233] like adoption into an Arab tribe in order to become a *mawla*, a client of the Islamic Arab patron and a member of the "central community" (*ummatan wasatan*) of believers. Martin comments:

> The strategy of recruitment for the fictive, as for natural, kinship societies was adoption, a legal fiction that permits kin relations to be created artificially, and which provided the model for the discourse of conversion and the practice of initiation in genealogically articulated systems. The Greek juridical term for adoption, *huiothesia*, is used in this derivative sense most notably by Paul.[234]

The initiate into the Eleusinian Mysteries, for example, is therefore regarded as a kinsman (*gennetes*) of the gods. The "mystery societies" were organised on the constitutional model of municipalities, and were not distinguished by their concealment of particular or extraordinary secrets, but by their pedagogical silence or "secrecy" (*arrhetos*)—even a real or pretended Socratic "ignorance"—as a rhetorical strategy

---

232. Sara Rappe, *Reading Neoplatonism: Non-discursive Thinking in the Texts of Plotinus, Proclus, and Damascius*, p. 164.
233. Luther H. Martin, *Secrecy in Hellenistic Religious Communities*, pp. 106-07.
234. *Ibid.*, pp. 105-106.

for structuring social relations in religious and educational contexts.[235]

The families of *telestai* that belonged to the groups (*thiasoi*) called *Orphikoi* viewed Dionysus as their *soter*; the Orphic *mustai* of Dionysus were promised *soteria* (salvation). In short, they were "initiates whom blessed Dionysus saves" (*mustai hous soze makar Dionusos*),[236] and they travelled the divine and royal path of purification, death and rebirth.

XXIII

Several teachings of Plato are based on Orphic and Pythagorean doctrines. It is, then, no wonder that even Socrates is portrayed by Plato as expecting after his death to meet Orpheus in Hades (*Apol.* 41a).

Some contemporary scholars argue that Plato, in certain cases, deliberately distorted, or rather reinterpreted and thus "modernised", the esoteric doctrines of Orpheus and Pythagoras. Ferwerda, for example, doubts that the Orphics (though surely craving for the liberation of the fettered soul) viewed the human body as a prison.[237] In *Cratylus* 400c, Plato states as follows:

> Some people maintain that the body (*soma*) is the tomb (*sema*) of the soul because the soul is buried there for this moment. And because, on the other hand, it indicates (*semainei*) by that body whatever the soul indicates, it is also for that reason rightly called sign (*sema*). However, it seems to me that Orpheus and his followers in the first place are the givers of that name (*soma*) because, in their opinion, the soul

235. *Ibid.*, p. 112.

236. Susan Guettel Cole, *Voices from beyond the Grave: Dionysus and the Dead*, p. 293.

237. Rein Ferwerda, *The Meaning of the Word* σῶμα *(Body) in the Axial Age: An Interpretation of Plato's CRATYLUS*, p. 122.

is being punished for something; the soul has the body as its enclosure (*peribolon*) in order to be saved (*hina sozetai),* just as a prison.

The word *soma* stands for the corpse in Homer, and only later acquires the meaning of body. So the following verse is attributed to Euripides by Plato: "Who knows whether living is not being dead, while being dead is living?" Plato's Socrates continues: "Perhaps we too are dead. I at least heard this from the wise men that now we are dead and that for us the body is a tomb" (*soma estin hemin sema*: *Gorg.* 492e-493a).

In his Commentary on Plato's Gorgias, Olympiodorus explains this as follows:

[Socrates] says "Euripides says to live is to die, and to die is to live." For on coming here, the soul, so that it may give life to the body, also gets a share in certain lifelessness. . . . So it is when it is separated that it is really alive. . . . The argument from the Pythagoreans is symbolic. For it employs a short myth, which says "We are dead here and we inhabit a tomb. . . . " (*In Gorg.* 29.4).[238]

The word *sema* principally stands for "sign" (*Odyssey* 20.111), therefore the body (*soma*) may be understood as a means by which the soul indicates (*semainei*) its eidetic paradigm and the goal to be achieved. Likewise, *sema* is an enclosure (*peribolos*), the morphic frame of the soul: it keeps the soul within its limits that it may be saved (*hina sozetai*).[239]

Microcosmically, this human body imitates the macrocosmic body of the Egyptian goddess Nut (Heaven), understood

238. *Olympiodorus' Commentary on Plato's Gorgias,* tr. Robin Jackson, Kimon Lycos and Harold Tarrant (Leiden: Brill, 1998), p. 206.
239. C.J. de Vogel, "The Soma-Sema Formula: Its Function in Plato and Plotinus Compared to Christian Writers," in *Neoplatonism and Early Christian Thought: Essays in honour of A. H. Armstrong,* ed. H.J. Blumenthal and R.A. Markus (London: Variorum Publications, 1981), pp. 80-81.

and depicted as the temple-like Duat, *mundus imaginalis*, into whose depths the ram-headed Ra descends as a *ba*-soul. The mummy (the completed and eternalised *sah*-body) inside the sarcophagus is an *imago* of Osiris. Therefore, the entire tomb of Osiris may be regarded as a symbol of spiritual alchemy.[240] According to Theodor Abt:

> The mummy that remains in the netherworld is called "the image of Osiris". As every deceased, man or woman, became an Osiris through the process of mummification, this mummy at the end of the Amduat is of course also the mummy of the dead person. Out of this "secret of the corpse", namely the unique individual image or structure of the deceased, the blessed immortal part became liberated by this journey through the twelve hours. He or she can now rise in the morning with the Sungod to immortality.[241]

The enclosure (*peribolos*)-like sarcophagus is sometimes protected by Isis and Nepthys at the corners at the head and Selket and Neith at those at the feet. The multi-structured tomb is like the House of Life (*per ankh*) which the goddess Seshat is said to open for the deceased. The sacred writings ("manifestations of Ra", *bau Ra*) are located in the animated House of Life as the recomposed *sah*-body of Osiris. Since in this respect writing and drawing are closely bound up with the dialectical and sacrificial dismembering and subsequent re-collection and resurrection of Osiris, the House of Life is both the sanctuary of the *bau* (*het bau*) and the place to die one's "philosophical death", that is, the Osirian netherworld which opens the road for one's spiritual journey:

---

240. Alison Roberts, *My Heart My Mother: Death and Rebirth in Ancient Egypt* (Rottingdean: Northgate Publishers, 2000), p. 203.
241. Theodor Abt and Erik Hornung, *Knowledge for the Afterlife: The Egyptian Amduat – A Quest for Immortality* (Zurich: Living Human Heritage Publications, 2003), p. 143.

In this way, the spiritual journey of the aspiring scribe may be described by images and terms drawn from the journey of the deceased in the underworld. . . . In P. Salt 825 the *per-ankh* of Abydos is said to consist of four parts, dedicated to Isis, Nepthys, Horus, and Thoth, while the interior is Osiris: "the living one."[242]

Consequently, for the ancient Egyptian initiates the "tomb" means an entirely different thing to what the majority of modern scholars imagine. The so-called "tomb", first of all, is the sanctuary-house by means of which the "living one" (the deceased) remains incorporated in the social net of the theophanic state. It is the *akhet* (a word deriving from the verb meaning "to be radiant", "to shine", "to make into a spirit of light"),[243] that is, the pyramid-like gate where the sun rises and the solar rebirth takes place. At the same time, it is the school of mystical pedagogy with its library and animated hieroglyphs—the divine speech fixed and eternalised in stone. As solidified light, the stone itself (as building material) refers to the primaeval *ben-ben* stone of Heliopolis. It is symbolically related with the royal conception of one's immortalisation through the ascent to heaven and inclusion within the circuit of Ra. The "tomb" is therefore *sema* in the sense of hieroglyph, the effective theurgic *sunthema*, like the Osirian *djed*-pillar or the solar obelisk standing on the primaeval mound. At the same time, it is the womb-like cave from which the restored Eye of Horus—the healed and restored initiate—emerges in the form of the golden Scarab.

---

242. Richard Jasnow and Karl-Theodor Zauzich, *The Ancient Egyptian Book of Thoth*, p. 35.
243. Jan Assmann, *The Mind of Egypt*, p. 58.

XXIV

It is plausible that various scattered Egyptian notions and images of the soul's immortality and ascent (through the alchemical descent to the Osirian Duat) were adapted and reused by the Orphics, Pythagoreans and Platonists. The association of heaven (in the sense of solar *kosmos noetos*) with immortality is an Egyptian theological doctrine, "occurring many millennia before it becomes part of Biblical or Greek tradition", according to Segal.[244] The winged *ba* of the pharaoh—the ideal *mer-rekh*, "lover of wisdom"—is transformed into the winged *akh* or the archetypal noetic star.

To indicate the ultimate Egyptian provenance of certain fundamental religious tendencies, patterns and ideas is not the same as to be passionately involved in a kind of "Platonic Orientalism", as analysed by John Walbridge.[245] At the same time, one needs to remember that "an afterlife belief" in its contemporary Western (or late antique) form "is not necessarily the essence of religion."[246] Or rather, it is not the explicit teaching of every ancient religion, including First and Second Temple Judaism (which Jacob Neusner emphasises in the plural).[247] "The Bible at first zealously ignores the afterlife."[248]

The Platonic Greek (and ultimately Egyptian) notion of the soul's immortality, its divine nature and its mystical union with the noetic or supra-noetic principle is very problematic even for early Christianity, which was initially a sectarian branch of late Second Temple ideologies and movements

---

244. Alan F. Segal, *Life after Death: A History of the Afterlife in Western Religion*, p. 38.

245. John Walbridge, *The Wisdom of the Mystic East: Suhrawardi and Platonic Orientalism* (Albany: State University of New York Press, 2001).

246. Alan F. Segal, *ibid.*, p. 17.

247. Jacob Neusner, Preface to *Judaisms and Their Messiahs at the Turn of the Christian Era*, ed. Jacob Neusner, William Scott Green and Ernest S. Frerichs (Cambridge: Cambridge University Press), p. IX.

248. Alan F. Segal, *ibid.*, p. 16.

based on the innovative rhetoric of the glorious resurrection promised for the Maccabean Jewish martyrs. But even this crucial doctrine rests on reshaped Graeco-Egyptian paradigms viewed through Persian lenses and attuned to Enochian apocalyptic expectations.

If all this seems unbelievable, or even offends certain romantic sensibilities, one should turn to W.K.C. Guthrie, L.J. Alderink and E.R. Dodds. But we do not belong to the camp of such respectable scholars as Dodds, whose knowledge "about early Orphism" diminished the more he read about it. He says: "I have lost a great deal of knowledge; for this loss I am indebted to Wilamowitz. . . . "[249]

This writer must confess to knowing very little as well—about either early Orphism or late Pythagoreanism. But I know that He-of-Heseret benefited my knowledge through madness, by diminishing it to such an extent that I cannot answer his question, "Who are you?" Perhaps I am the mummy-like jackal who has come from the four corners of Nun and wishes to bark among the dogs of Seshat.

M.L. West says that "scholars sometimes choose to believe strange things."[250] And he himself becomes a primary example of this bizarre phenomenon, arguing that "Olympiodorus' interpretation of the Orphic myth is to be rejected,"[251] because it is a "merely Neoplatonist interpretation".[252] When the Orphic and Bakchic *sunthemata* are handed down in the rites of the Orphics and the symbolic story of the dismemberment is enacted, for West, all this merely offers "temporary escape from ordinary life into a piquant, romantic, voluptuous fantasy-world".[253]

---

249. E.R. Dodds, *The Greeks and the Irrational* (Berkeley: University of California Press, 1951), p. 147.
250. M.L. West, *The Orphic Poems*, p. 45.
251. *Ibid.*, p. 166.
252. *Ibid.*, p. 164.
253. *Ibid.*, pp. 173-74.

Finally, Larry Alderink comes up with the last judgement, that any claims about an "alleged Orphic afterlife" or the idea of post-mortem existence as *telos* are obscure, questionable and inconclusive.[254]

---

254. Larry J. Alderink, *Creation and Salvation in Ancient Orphism*, p. 3.

OTHER TITLES BY ALGIS UŽDAVINYS

The Golden Chain: An Anthology of Platonic and Pythagorean Philosophy
(World Wisdom, 2004)

Philosophy as a Rite of Rebirth: From Ancient Egypt to Neoplatonism
(The Matheson Trust and Prometheus Trust, 2004)

The Heart of Plotinus: The Essential Enneads
(World Wisdom, 2009)

Philosophy and Theurgy in Late Antiquity
(Sophia Perennis, 2010)

Ascent to Heaven in Islamic and Jewish Mysticism
(The Matheson Trust, 2011)

ORIGINAL LITHUANIAN WORKS
(forthcoming in English from The Matheson Trust)

Labyrinth of Sources. Hermeneutical Philosophy and Mystagogy of Proclus
(Vilnius, 2002)

Hellenic Philosophy from Numenius to Syrianus
(Vilnius, 2003)

Hermes Trismegistus: The Way of Wisdom
(Vilnius, 2005)